# An Introduction to
# CROP CIRCLES

## Andy Thomas

## Contents

## WESSEX BOOKS
*www.wessexbooks.co.uk*

*Crop circle near the ancient site of Adam's Grave, Alton Barnes, Wiltshire, 2007*

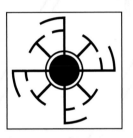

*Crop circles are a global phenomenon; this design appeared at Ostrava in the Czech Republic in 1998*

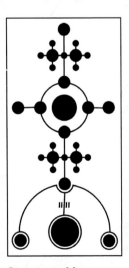

*Pictogram at Manton, Wiltshire, 4 May 2009*

An unmistakable air of mystery surrounds certain parts of southern England, especially counties such as Wiltshire, places that were once part of the ancient kingdom of Wessex. This region has long been home to the unusual and unexplained. Believed by many to be the ancient land of King Arthur himself, the Wessex landscape embraces the Stonehenge and Avebury stone circles, the enigmatic Silbury Hill and hundreds of ancient burial mounds. It also plays host to scores of UFO sightings, reports of mysterious black cats and dogs, covens, ghosts and, most famously, crop circles, those increasingly elaborate shapes found swirled into fields each summer.

Crop circles – also known as corn circles, crop formations, crop glyphs or agriglyphs – were first brought to wider public attention in the 1980s, but there is clear evidence of them at least as far back as 1678. Although two-thirds of circular activity occurs in England, crop circles are found all over the world. Many other countries have reported events, including, more prominently, Italy, Germany, Canada, The Netherlands, the Czech Republic, Australia, Switzerland, Poland, Russia and the USA.

Formations can be found etched into many types of crops, and laid down in either a clockwise, anticlockwise or even radial fashion. Wheat and barley fields are the most commonly visited, but oilseed rape (canola), rye, oats, maize, flax, peas and various other plants have also been known to host designs. Natural mediums have been utilised by the phenomenon too, amongst them grassland, bracken and heather. In Britain, the majority of crop circles appear within the county of Wiltshire, but other areas have also received their fair share, with prominent examples including Hampshire, Oxfordshire, Bedfordshire, East and West Sussex, Warwickshire, North and South Yorkshire, the East Midlands, and as far north as Scotland.

This book exists to give a brief, yet insightful, overview of the crop circle phenomenon – the history, the development of the patterns, and the possible theories which might explain them. While not intended as a definitive study (some excellent books and websites for the more dedicated researcher are listed under *Further Information*), it hopefully serves as a good introduction to something far more complex and intriguing than most people are aware of.

What the crop circle mystery has done, above all, is to provide a fascinating forum of debate about the nature of reality and the mysterious world around us, as both sceptics and mystics strive to prove their cases. Indeed, the continuing *absence* of a definitive answer to the circles has stimulated an unexpected deepening of thought in many people as they grapple with the issues and strange matters arising from this compelling and yet frustratingly elusive phenomenon. ◉

The Stonehenge Fractal
This staggering formation appeared on 7 July 1996 and remains a highlight of the phenomenon. One of a series of 'fractal' shapes (self-replicating patterns which result from natural reiterative equations, as generated by computers), this design is known as a 'Julia Set'. Evidence shows that this huge glyph, 915 feet long and comprising 151 circles, appeared in daylight hours within a period of 45 minutes [pages 18 & 36] in full view of Stonehenge and the A303 road – with no-one being seen in the vicinity.

Unable to stop visitors entering the field, the farmer charged an admission fee (largely donated to a local charity) and advertised the formation on the roadside. This policy, at such a tourist spot, led to it becoming the most visited crop circle in history, with an estimated 10,000 people passing through it during the course of that summer

# 1: What are Crop Circles?

*Inside a crop circle near the Cherhill white horse carving, Wiltshire, 1992*

The lack of physical evidence in paranormal mysteries has always been frustrating for researchers, whether studying the Loch Ness Monster, ghosts, Bigfoot or UFOs. Crop formations present the exact opposite of this – the evidence arrives on a regular basis, in stunning and beautiful form for all to see. Paradoxically, this undeniable presence has almost certainly increased the controversy around them, with detailed examinations (and subsequent heated discussions) easily available to all, not just the lucky few. We shall explore the arguments about man-made versus mysterious later, but most open-minded observers accept that at least a proportion of formations cannot be explained by human activity.

While some formations are just a few feet across and simple, the vast majority are now highly sophisticated patterns and generally span hundreds (occasionally thousands) of feet. Although tractor lines cross most English fields (the stripes visible in aerial photos), agriglyphs have also been found in the middle of farmland without them, with no visible trails leading in. They are mostly placed fully within the selected field, although boundaries and even roads have been crossed on noted occasions, with one large ring in 1993 at West Overton, Wiltshire, encompassing three fields around an entire T-junction.

*Looking across a huge pentagram formation at Beckhampton, Wiltshire, 8 August 1998*

Most of the more 'intelligent'-looking crop glyphs seem ambiguous in their symbolism, but more direct ones have alluded to everything from ancient or religious iconography to modern scientific and

astronomical data, sparking many discussions about their origins. Some designs embody incredibly complex geometrical features and display mathematical qualities beyond pure chance or haphazard placement. Books and papers have been inspired by these elements alone, and the late Professor Gerald S Hawkins (famous for decoding the geometrical layout of Stonehenge) even derived a whole new mathematical theorem

*This astonishing 194-circle fractal design appeared at Windmill Hill, Avebury, Wiltshire, 29 July 1996*

based on observing the diatonic ratios embodied in crop circles. In addition to the geometry, complexity is often found in the laid crop itself, with layered flows, swirls and weaves. Other notable physical features can include biological anomalies in circle-affected crop (absent in known man-made designs), suggesting some kind of heating or energy process at work.

Despite many crop circles seemingly being created at night, apparently in the pre-dawn early hours, there have been a number of proven daylight occurrences (sometimes with eye-witnesses), and large designs have arrived within very short periods of time. Although similar patterns have been known to form in less visible mediums at other times of the year – ice, snow and earth circles have all been reported – the vast majority of crop designs are found between April and September in the UK (with seasonal variations in other parts of the world), the peak months being July and August, and the epicenter of English – indeed global – activity being around Avebury and Silbury Hill. Local weather conditions do not seem to be a major factor in their arrival, as they are known to appear in rain and fog as well as clear conditions, and there is no obvious correlation with lunar or astrological cycles influencing individual appearances.

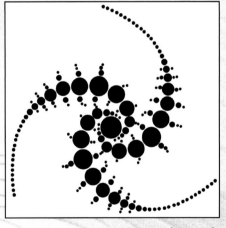

*Seen as a diagram, the mathematical genius of the Windmill Hill design can be more fully appreciated*

Although crop circles have been found on many types of soil worldwide, it is an interesting fact that the vast majority of English formations appear to arrange themselves in direct conjunction with aquiferous rocks – strata which carry large volumes of underground water. Mapping out the distribution of the circles onto geological charts makes this connection undeniable, with chalk appearing to be the primary attractor for the Wessex examples. Circles in other countries have similar correlations with their regional aquifers. The geological connection would seem to be an important factor in the placement of formations. As water is known to create energetic effects in the ground, a natural component may contribute to the process of circle creation, whatever other causes may be involved. Of course, many believe there to be an intelligent impetus of some kind that must also play a part, as will be discussed further under *Theories and Beliefs*.

*The ancient mound of Silbury Hill at Avebury, Wiltshire is the precise epicentre of global crop circle activity. Its origin and purpose is unknown – like the circles that cluster around it. Could geology have played a role in the placement of Neolithic sites – and could it also be influencing the distribution of the circles? The evidence suggests so*

The circle mystery is certainly multi-layered. All manner of peripheral anomalous phenomena have been reported in and around crop glyphs over the years. Most notably, aerial lights have often been seen coming down into fields where new formations are subsequently discovered, and floating balls of light have been witnessed, and filmed, on numerous occasions in and around existing patterns. Whether the circlemaking process originates in the sky, or from the earth, or is a combination of both, isn't yet known, but eye-witnesses often speak of a descending presence. On occasions when crop circles arrive, there have also been reports of buzzing electronic sounds, very high-pitched whistling/trilling effects, and even loud roaring.

*Right: This beautiful design at Roundway, Wiltshire, appeared on 31 July 1999 and exhibited some of the best lay patterns then seen in a formation*

We will explore all of these aspects and much more throughout these pages. ◉

*An insect-like winged formation below the white horse carving at Milk Hill, Alton Barnes, Wiltshire, 26 June 2004*

# 2: Inside a Formation

*The welcome sight of a farmer's donation box, indicating that circle visitors can enter in peace. Going in without permission is illegal!*

The Internet now makes it very easy to find crop circles to visit. News of the latest arrivals is usually posted within hours, with information on their general locations freely available. Once in the vicinity, advice from locals or the simple presence of other seekers can give useful pointers as to where to go. Crop fields are, it should be remembered, private land, and permission should always be sought to walk in unless the farmer has placed a donation box at the entrance to the field, in which case one can explore in a more assured state. Entering without permission can lead to tension and inevitable altercations with farm staff. Once the location of a formation is clearly identified and it can be seen from the ground (any hillsides are obviously helpful for this), visitors must choose carefully which tractor line to enter by. Walking *through* the crop is not an option and perpetrated only by the unthinking – and uncaring. Fields can be much larger than they seem from a distance and miscalculating the entrance point can lead to long double-backs, so care should be taken. Friendly farmers usually denote which track to use, or the main trodden paths soon make themselves apparent.

The (sometimes long) walk into a field is finally rewarded by the unique and humbling experience of entering the crop circle itself. Often invisible during the walk up the tractor line, quite suddenly the laid area opens up as a vast new enclosure in what was once a featureless sea of unaffected stems. A huge swirl invites the visitor in, or side paths and other avenues may present multiple choices of areas to explore. Ground exploration has been likened to walking a sacred maze or labyrinth. Indeed, some see crop glyphs as sacred places for the modern age, and it cannot be denied that there is something

*Maze-like pathways at Roundway, Wiltshire, 25 July 2010*

cathedral-like about the feeling of standing in a vast complex of sophisticated geometry with a wide open space above.

Crop circles are remarkable for their crisp, sharp edges, and flattened but often undamaged stems. The circle wall is usually clearly

*Sweeping flows of very tidy crop at Alton Priors, Wiltshire, 23 July 2008*

demarked, with little overspill into the surrounding area, although on occasion an intriguing interface of standing and laid plants interlaced together at the edge makes clear that something far more subtle than a basic manual implement has been at work. In a good formation, the stems in the main lay will be neatly flattened to the ground, flowing around exquisitely, almost with a fluid motion. Lifting up layers going in one direction can sometimes reveal flows beneath, running in counter-directions, while other areas may show complex weaves where flows meet. Man-made demonstrations have struggled to replicate these features. Some circles are clockwise, some anticlockwise, with no seeming preference, and many multi-circled designs will incorporate both kinds. Radial lays have also been known, flowing inward or outward. Although the plants may be lying horizontally, they still grow and ripen without any apparent harm. Sometimes, without too many visitors, crop will recover, to stand straight again after a few days.

A variety of swirled centres can be found in crop formations, some wide splays, others coned upwards, and others still with a central standing tuft. Tightly knotted and woven features have also become more common in recent years. Often, it is hard to understand from

*Many kinds of centres can be found in different crop circles. To the left, a flattened, swirled variety can be seen, at Patcham, near Brighton, East Sussex, in 1992, while below is a coned example, leaving an impressive deep central hole, in the Milk Hill 'Koch fractal' of 1997 [page 26]*

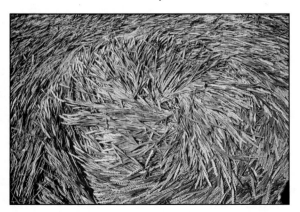

the ground what the overall shape of the glyph is, unless it has already been viewed from the air. All that can be seen inside are circles, paths and shapes of various sizes running off in every direction. Walking through

Above & right: *A great variety of circle centres can be found, from standing tufts of crop to twisted or tightly-knotted craftwork*

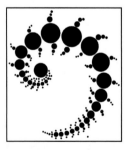

*The Stonehenge fractal of 1996 [page 3] saw a spate of health effects on visitors, including a number of women who found their menstrual cycles disrupted!*

a formation can be an exciting, mysterious and hypnotic delight.

But there is more to being inside a crop circle than may at first be apparent – thus, a word of warning. A significant number of people entering them have reported experiencing a variety of physical and mental effects. Depending on the formation, and on the individual, these can range from feelings of elation and peacefulness, to nausea, headaches, disorientation and panic. Some have reported electrical tingles and other odd sensations. There have been notable cases of the health of visitors seemingly being affected by the circles in a profound way. 'Miracles' and healings have been reported, but also sudden declines in well-being, as well as menstrual cycles being disrupted. Animals have also been known to behave very strangely in and around crop circles, and livestock and local dogs have been known to react wildly in fields or houses near new arrivals.

There may be more to this than imagination, as it is not just organic material that is vulnerable. Electronic equipment, for instance, seems to malfunction far above the dictates of statistical chance when taken inside formations, with regular reports of mobile phone batteries draining and cameras failing, together with strange effects on compasses and other magnetic devices. There have been several occasions where TV news crews have been frustrated when equipment has failed to work. Farmers have also reported combine harvesters breaking down when attempting to cut circles (as, inevitably, all formations meet their end when the harvest comes).

A number of causes have been put forward to account for these quirks. It is possible that the electrical qualities of the aforementioned underground water and geological 'earth energies' may be coming into play, but everything from natural magnetism, piezoelectrics, unearthly energy fields and psychic forces have all been suggested as culprits. Some health problems may also be caused by the ubiquitous presence of pesticides - or by simple cases of sunstroke. But others point out that the power of shape itself has traditionally been seen as a generator of strong mystical experiences, so perhaps the cause of these reports is a combination of several elements, with the designs somehow amplifying the consequences. Some people can explore a formation and feel positive, whilst others may have a negative emotion – perhaps the circles simply enhance the state with which one goes into the field. Either way, it should be clearly understood that one enters a crop circle at one's own risk!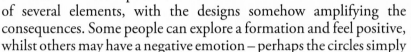

*Several TV camera crews – even sceptical ones – have reported inexplicable malfunctioning of electronic equipment inside circles*

Left: *Flows of crop spilling from a pathway at Patcham, East Sussex, 29 June 1992*

Below: *Many people report health effects, good and bad, whilst or after visiting formations. Do the patterns amplify natural energy?*

*A ring in crop at Bow Hill, near Chichester, West Sussex, 1932 (bottom of picture), as reproduced in* Sussex Notes and Queries *(1934), the earliest likely photo of a simple formation. Although some thought it to be an archaeological 'hut mark', the crop is clearly described as being 'beaten down'*

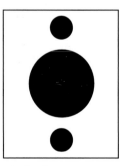

*The first formation to gain national attention, at Cheesefoot Head, Hampshire, 1981*

Contrary to popular perception, crop circles are not a new phenomenon. Some believe they may have been part of the landscape since ancient times. A large proportion of crop patterns regularly appear in or around an area that has become known as the 'Wessex Triangle', with its main cardinal points around Silbury Hill, Warminster, and Winchester. The Triangle boasts the presence of England's largest stone circles, at Avebury and Stonehenge. The whole region is littered with burial mounds, many also circular. Silbury is the largest man-made earthwork in Europe, its source and purpose, like the crop circles, still a complete mystery. Considering the grandeur and sheer number of these ancient round constructions, some have postulated that awestruck Neolithic farmers may have seen crop circles thousands of years ago and built their temples on those spots to commemorate them. It is interesting to note that there have been some curious connections between the layout of stone circles and the geometry found in agriglyphs.

Though it is clear that there are far more crop circles today, and they have clearly evolved in complexity, some modern farmers recall having seen them in fields all their lives, as did their parents and grandparents. The earliest known photo of an apparent crop circle is from 1932, near Bow Hill, Chichester, in West Sussex [see left]. In general, it seems that they weren't widely reported in earlier times, either through fear or superstition, or because they were simply considered the result of animals or wind. Crows were likely suspects for rougher areas, and 'circular damage' might also have been thought to be the result of rare crop diseases, which the owner would certainly not want to advertise. However, for the clearer markings, there is evidence to show that before the 1900s crop circles might have been attributed to fairies - or the Devil, as in the famous 1678 woodcut seen on the opposite page. The accompanying text of this illustration makes plain that something very close to our modern phenomenon was occurring even then. The pamphlet's description of the sky being 'all of a flame' on the night of the supposedly demonic events sounds strongly like the anomalous aerial lights still being seen in association with crop circles today [page 37].

However, despite a growing record of circular happenings throughout the 20th century, particularly in the 1960s (including photos of 'UFO

# The Mowing - Devil :

## Or, Strange NEWS out of

# Hartford - ſhire.

Being a True Relation of a Farmer, who Bargaining
with a Poor Mower, about the Cutting down Three Half
Acres of Oats; upon the Mower's asking too much, the Farmer wore, That the Devil ſhould Mow it, rather than He
And ſo it fell out, that that very Night, the Crop of Oat
Drew'd as if it had been all of a Flame; but next Morning
appear'd ſo neatly Mow'd by the Devil, or ſome Infernal Spi-
rit, that no Mortal Man was able to do the like.
Alſo, How the ſaid Oats ly now in the Field, and the Owner
has not Power to fetch them away.

Licenſed, Auguſt 22th, 1678.

nests' in Queensland, Australia in 1966) and 1970s (increasingly in England), the first crop formation to attract the serious attention of the British media was the line of three circles found at Cheesefoot Head, Hampshire, in July 1981. The central circle measured 55 feet, with the smaller ones measuring 26 feet each; small by today's standards, but significant then. Researchers of countryside curiosities had been studying single circles for a few years at this point, but with little interest from the press. After the Cheesefoot Head event, though publicised reports were still sparse for a while, interest began to grow,

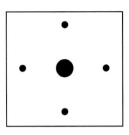

*'Quintuplets' (as at Beckhampton, Wiltshire, 1988, above), eventually developed into 'Celtic crosses' (Sompting, West Sussex, 1999, middle), and culminated in this incredible 'cross of Celtic crosses' at Avebury, 27 July 2005*

and enthusiasts such as Pat Delgado, Colin Andrews and meteorologist Terence Meaden gradually found themselves becoming the first spokesmen for this 'new' mystery. As single circles continued to be found, a strange evolution of form also made itself known. It didn't take long before doubles, triplets and 'quintuplets' began to show up in fairly rapid succession. Concentric rings also began to feature more regularly, and in 1986 the 'Celtic cross' configuration made its first appearance. In 1988, around 75 circles were reported, creating an annual UK average that has remained reasonably steady since.

The last formation of 1989, at Winterbourne Stoke, Wiltshire, on 12 August, suggested that something new was about to develop – a single circle with crop swept in four quartered directions could surely not be considered a simple weather effect, as had largely been thought until then. Indeed, this subtle hint blossomed into full-blown shock in 1990. The first 'pictograms' – long hieroglyphic chains of circles and rings combined with rectangles and other shapes – began to appear, and soon became the national standard. Now anything was possible. After a brief honeymoon period of media excitement, the widely-publicised hoax claims of 'Doug and Dave' in 1991 [page 17] distracted the masses for a while, but did little to halt the remarkable progression of the designs nor dented the interest of those able to see beyond the one-sided sceptic propaganda of cynical journalists. In the decades since, the ever-more elaborate and astonishing designs

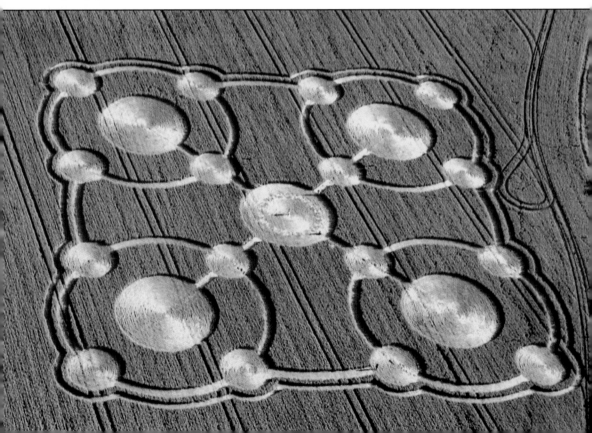

which have occurred have taken the phenomenon to new heights and controversies that no one could have guessed at in the early years [see *The Evolution of the Designs*], taking many observers on an extraordinary journey of enchantment and confusion, which continues to this day.

A fuller history of the crop circles can be found in the *Crop Circle Timeline* on page 49. ◉

Crop flows around a corner at Roundway, Wiltshire, 25 July 2010

A 'mandala'-type design (with a companion in the distance), at Alton Barnes, Wiltshire, 6 August 2001

A single standing stem of oats left at the centre of an ellipse at Lewes, East Sussex, 14 June 2003

Crop flows smoothly to a point at Alton Priors, Wiltshire, 23 July 2008

*Two formations at Avebury, Wiltshire, 2 June 2002.*

# 4: Mysterious or Man-Made?

The greatest arguments over crop circles have concerned their origins – and whether they are the product of some unknown force or simply man-made art. Though uninformed opinion and the narrow propaganda of the media tends toward the latter as the sole cause, many others believe that a significant proportion of formations demands a better explanation. We shall explore some of the non-human possibilities under *Theories and Beliefs*.

Of the known hoaxers there have been, the first to claim authorship were a pair of elderly gentlemen named Doug Bower and Dave Chorley who came forward in 1991. Doug and Dave claimed the whole thing started as a joke that then got out of hand. Their creations were flattened using a plank held with a piece of rope, and later with garden rollers. Public interest in the circles was undoubtedly dented by the wide and gloating media coverage given to the pensioners, but actual evidence for any spectacular works was notably absent, while their demonstrations resulted in heavily damaged plants and were geometrically poor. These weak efforts and the entirely unsubstantiated story left their claims looking highly suspicious and failed to account for the large numbers of formations over the years, nor explained the historical or overseas reports. Indeed, some believe Doug and Dave were a deliberate 'distraction' created to dilute the interest in a real phenomenon, a theory given more credence when it turned out that the press agency ('MBF Services'), which put their original story out, did not actually exist. When researchers tried to track it down, the only available contacts appeared to have curious links to the British intelligence services, leaving some understandably dubious about the entire Doug and Dave circus.

Other 'artists' have since come forward to insinuate that they or their kind make all the crop circles but, in comparison to the more mysterious designs, their demonstrations are typically less impressive and are rarely made within the same time frame and circumstances, with none of the unusual or intricate effects often observed. The long sessions – on occasion, six to nine hours or more – taken to create even fairly modest crop formations by human teams in public demonstrations throw marked doubt on the notion that all patterns are man-made. A car-shaped emblem created by a team of more experienced crop artists ('The Circlemakers') for a Mitsubishi advert in 1998 reportedly took two days to construct, in broad daylight and with no need of time-consuming stealth – yet several glyphs often arrive in a single night, sometimes across two or three counties, when even one would be more than a night's work based on the evidence from the human circlemakers. With numerous designs arriving in fields close to roads that can already

*Martinsell Hill, Wiltshire, 19 July 2007*

*Boxley, Kent, 8 July 2006*

*Clatford, Wiltshire, 9 August 2008*

*Alton Barnes, Wiltshire, 3 July 2005*

*An array of extraordinary crop formations. Can all of these simply be the result of people with planks and ropes, as the media insists?*

*Unusual – and difficult to execute – 'parabolic' curves make up this unique design at Blowingstone Hill, Uffington, Oxfordshire, 6 August 2006*

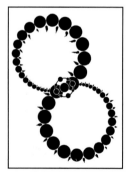

*Some designs are notable for not being witnessed forming: this apt figure-of-eight appeared at Milk Hill, Wiltshire, on 8 August 2008 (8/8/08). Despite a nearby mass-meditation, nothing was seen or heard that night [page 54]*

be busy by dawn, it seems likely that any teams still working away (as they would sometimes need to be given the demonstrated time-frames) should have been easily caught many times by now, yet this rarely seems to happen.

A significant number of designs are known to have appeared within very short periods of time, sometimes in daylight hours and in very public places, as at Stonehenge in 1996, where a 915 feet-long fractal pattern arrived within a forty-five minute window in full view of the A303 road at around 5.30pm – with no-one being seen [page 3]. Stonehenge security guards, farm staff and a pilot testify that the field had been empty up until that time. Sightings of aerial phenomena and actual eye-witness accounts of circles forming also challenge the total-hoax view [see *Eye Witnesses and Experiences*]. With an incredible 10,000 or so recorded crop formations, it is notable that there has only ever been one prosecution against a human circle-creator, despite several police enquiries and offered rewards for the capture of illegal artists.

Overall, the bottom line in deciding whether the whole phenomenon is merely creative japery or not must surely be decided by comparing known man-made designs with the qualities found in those of unknown origin. Incredibly – and manipulatively – there is usually almost no discussion at all of any of the key criteria when television programmes or journalists attempt to dismiss the accumulated evidence of a more extraordinary cause. Although human artists have undoubtedly honed their skills as years have gone by, the layered, intricate and largely undamaged flow of crop inside many patterns is still at odds with most demonstrations carried out with planks and ropes over the years, when the fine detail is examined. These often show poor construction, footprints and dirt on stems, broken plants, holes in the ground, or disturbances in the crop where poles or people have been used as pivots. When examined closely and carefully, regular thin white crease marks on young stems are also found in nearly all man-made formations, created every few feet where the planks of wood break the stems at regular intervals – yet such marks seem to be absent in a significant number of the anonymous masterpieces. In addition, many plants, when young and green, have a delicate silvery bloom (a fine white film) that grows on them. When touched even lightly, this bloom can be removed and, when trodden down, the scuffing and blemishes in it are plain

*Close-up of a man-made formation created for a TV programme. Regular white crease marks and scuffing of the 'bloom', as seen here, are evident in most manually-flattened crop circles*

to see – despite this, a large number of crop formations show no such physical traces. Just the footwear of visitors can leave clear markings on plants, yet many brand new lays are entirely pristine when first entered. This is very noticeable in wet conditions, where mud is soon plastered everywhere by the first of the investigators, in what was until then clean and unmarked crop.

The bending of certain stem-types can be another important criterion for consideration. In many rapeseed (canola) designs, for instance, plants can be found bent neatly to the ground, and yet few are broken or dead. This is especially hard to accomplish in rape, which has the consistency of celery and snaps easily – yet many examples have been found bent at 90 degree angles. Nodal bending is another phenomenon hard to explain. Wheat-type plants are sometimes found bent at the nodal joints (the 'knuckles' of the stems) to create certain shapes in the lay, or to enable them to flow around corners. This is an impossible feat in manually-flattened crop, never yet found in a man-made pattern. Only the natural effects of 'gravitropism' or 'phototropism' can achieve this, as stems dry out or grow back towards the light from the node; but this is not what is found in formations, where the stems are clearly laid in that fashion from the very start.

*Bent and swollen nodes help create curvature within some crop lays, yet seem to be absent in man-made designs*

How, then, are the plants bent in some cases? One non-human theory is that the circle-forming process somehow heats the crop. Exhaustive lab analysis into hundreds of crop circles carried out by

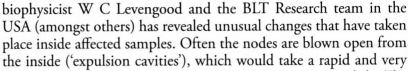

biophysicist W C Levengood and the BLT Research team in the USA (amongst others) has revealed unusual changes that have taken place inside affected samples. Often the nodes are blown open from the inside ('expulsion cavities'), which would take a rapid and very brief rate of heating to accomplish. The seed cavities and nodes are often elongated or mutated, and abnormal developments in the germination rate of the seeds themselves have been noted. These results suggest the possibility that the plants have been exposed to short, intense bursts of microwave radiation. (This may be another explanation for those who display symptoms of negative effects after spending time in formations.) No known man-made patterns have shown any such biological changes, and yet the majority of tested samples *have* shown these results. Sceptics have inevitably attacked the biological analyses as flawed, but it is interesting to note that they nearly always try to achieve this by misrepresenting the results, attacking the personalities, or by omitting important data. However, both Levengood and the Dutch astrophysicist Eltjo Haselhoff have had papers on changes to circle-affected stems published in the scientific peer-review journal *Physiologia Plantarum*, and this kind of work deserves far more coverage and discussion. Other related tests suggest a source that descends from high in the atmosphere, a theory derived from the traces of meteoritic dust and other stratospheric deposits that have been found on some stems (this would fit with some of the eye-witness accounts of vortex-like 'tubes' descending from the sky).

*A visitor to a formation discovers double bent nodes. Bending plants at the node is impossible with any known manual technique*

*Crooked Soley, Wiltshire, 27 August 2002. The brilliantly complex geometry of this design inspired a whole book on it [page 55]*

Aside from the physical effects, from a design point of view, a large number of crop patterns are near-perfection, with sharp edges and a staggering geometrical precision [see opposite], allowing accurate sacred numerical information and even astronomical data to be laid in the fields. The mathematics and geometry of crop formations have been the subjects of academic study. Known man-made efforts always seem to fall down by comparison, or take an unrealistically long time to construct. Artists have learned to make their work look pretty, and therefore perhaps convincing to novices, but 'planked' formations so often do not embody the complexity and subtlety of the more mysterious patterns, as analyses and comparisons have shown.

Beyond the rather unscientific, though not necessarily unreliable, method of simply sensing which formations 'feel' right, there have been many attempts to establish 'litmus tests', but simple discernment

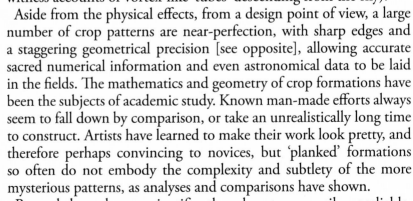

*Exquisite meeting flows of crop at Roundway, Wiltshire, 25 July 2010*

# Crop Circle Geometry

**Diagrams revealing the ingenious and highly accurate geometrical construction of three formations. All diagrams and analysis by ALLAN BROWN ©**

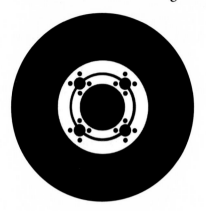 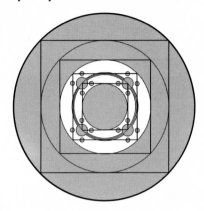

Telegraph Hill, Hampshire, 12 June 1995. The geometry is made up of four nested squares. The inner two squares define the positions of the large and small satellites

Bishops Cannings, Wiltshire, 13 July 1997. This is made up from a series of pentagram relationships, with the centre defined by nested pentagons

 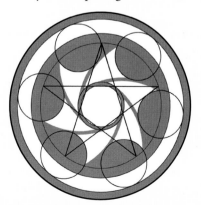

Etchilhampton, Wiltshire, 1 August 1997. A pentagram defines the outside edge of the inner ring. The ring is then used to define the curve of the 'rotating' arms, which then defines the inside edge of the formation's outer ring

*A stunning mandala of 'cubes' and triangles at Sugar Hill, Upper Upham, Wiltshire, 1 August 2007. How easy would this be to lay out in a field at night?*

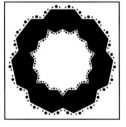

*Impressive aerial lights were seen coming down into the field the night this design arrived at Tawsmead Copse, Alton Priors, Wiltshire, 9 August 1998. Human circlemakers have also claimed to have seen such lights*

and observation is often the most valuable tool. However, various detection techniques have been tried, including the ancient art of dowsing, using rods and pendulums [page 41]. Dowsers believe non-man-made crop circles emit particular energy patterns, while manually-laid pictograms have more basic properties, or produce no results at all. Some claim that the very act of making circles, at least in certain specific areas, can actually change the energy patterns in the locale, but dowsers say they can detect the difference.

Sometimes the attraction of investigating how crop circles could be made has become too great, and there have been cases of serious researchers who have 'gone to the other side' and become human circlemakers themselves. There can also be money in commercial crop circles, as the self-named 'Circlemakers' team have proved, by making numerous demonstrations for television programmes and advertisements. Yet, given that most demo formations are so often paid for handsomely by the media, it is interesting to note that most of these seem to be made by varied combinations from the same pool of just five or six people, all of whom could not possibly account for more than a modest proportion of the thousands of formations that have arrived over the years. One has to wonder where all the other mysterious artists are and why they don't try to capitalise on their craft in the same way. Inside knowledge of other secret circle artists is often claimed by sceptics, but very rarely is any evidence for these people produced.

Nevertheless, some of the human circlemakers that there are say that they feel they are creating sacred art. Others claim that while they make their formations they have a sense of being watched and protected by a higher intelligence, and they themselves have sometimes reported seeing strange aerial lights and have experienced other inexplicable phenomena. Few of them would boast that they can explain everything about crop circles. Even Doug Bower stated that he and Dave Chorley might have been used by a higher power while they were making their crop circles, though many felt this to be a smokescreen of cynical mysticism to blur the arguments against them.

Nearly all people today accept that a percentage of each year's crop glyphs are man-made, though most would be hard pushed to prove in what proportion, as the phenomenon seems to be forever elusive in providing hard evidence in that direction, certainty always dancing away from researchers, rather than toward them. Human circlemaking has clearly been developed over the years, and with enough time and effort reasonable simulations have been made – yet many formations simply cannot be explained this way. To say that *all* crop circles are man-made is to ignore the evidence, much of which suggests something far stranger at work. Perhaps the best thing to conclude is to state the old adage: one counterfeit coin does not mean that all coins are counterfeit. ◎

*Knotted centres at Windmill Hill, Avebury, Wiltshire, 27 July 2010. 'Believers' say these are hard to achieve by hand without causing overt damage, but sceptics disagree. Yet demonstrations never seem to solve the arguments*

*'Nautilus' shell at Pewsey, Wiltshire, 17 July 2002, created using exquisite mathematical steps. The small circle to the upper right was originally a tiny replica of the main design, but was quickly wrecked by visitors. Walking around crop is hard to do without causing damage*

PHILOSOPHI. ASTRONOMI. ALCHIMI. VIRTVTES.

CABALA

The Barbury Triangle

The glyph which appeared at Barbury Castle on 17 July 1991 featured a triangle (or possibly a representation of a tetrahedron) with sides measuring about 180 feet, on top of which was a massive double-ringed circle. Situated at the points of the triangle were three symbols, almost 90 feet across, each of a different design. It became one of the most famous formations of the early 1990s.

Its three circles within a triangle evoke echoes of the power of three, the 'Triune', held in much respect by religion and especially practitioners of the arts of alchemy and sacred geometry. Indeed, it is strikingly similar to an illustration in a 1654 book on the Qabala (an ancient mystical belief), Cabala, Speculum Altis et Naturae in Alchymia [inset], where it represents the Tree of Life, or the cosmic egg, in the process of creation.

The majestic glyph was situated in a place of ancient power, and certain events that occurred close to the time of its creation, including a loud roaring noise and strange shapes/ lights in the sky, lent it a further air of mystery

# 5: The Evolution of the Designs

O ne of the most fascinating – and controversial – aspects of the circle mystery is the obvious fact that the patterns have changed and evolved over the years.

In the 1970s, the crop circles were largely just that – circles, whether single or in various combinations of clustered sizes. But from the end of that decade onwards, more patterns known as 'quintuplets' began to arrive, four small satellites around a central larger circle. As the 1980s progressed, rings developed, eventually combining with quintuplets to produce 'Celtic cross' designs.

The years from the first pictograms of 1990 saw the most significant development, and thus a big change occurred in the way the circles were perceived, for now they seemed more like *designs*, incorporating circles, arcs, rectangles, straight paths and many other components. Insect-like shapes with curly features began to appear in 1991 and other 'animal' genres included a number of abstract whale-like symbols. In the same year, one of the most spectacular pictograms ever seen appeared on 17 July in a field below the ancient hill-fort of Barbury Castle, near Swindon, Wiltshire, being a triangular representation of a tetrahedron tipped with cryptic symbols at each point [see opposite]. It was by now clear that we were dealing with something capable of great sophistication, and therefore not simply a random weather phenomenon as some had postulated.

A depiction of a 'Mandelbrot Set', the first truly recognisable design to appear, was found on 12 August 1991, at Ickleton, near Cambridge. Devised from the computer-driven science of 'fractals' (self-replicating shapes creating infinite dimensions), a Mandelbrot Set is one of the most complex mathematical constructs, used sometimes to demonstrate how order arises automatically from chaos. Were the makers of this formation asking us to consider the fine line between chaos and order? Was it a warning that if humankind continued its destructive ways, it would cross the line into chaos? Or was it just a naturally-produced shape, a true fractal [page 39]?

The representations of astronomical events were perhaps the most outstanding move forward. The aptly-named 'galaxy' designs of 1994, for instance, were later found to be clear depictions of a planetary alignment in the constellation Cetus, which would occur on 6 April 2000 [next page]. When the predicted date finally arrived, one of the largest solar storms in years erupted, creating spectacular displays of the *aurora borealis* across countries which normally wouldn't see it. Coincidence or prediction? Other astronomical diagrams in the fields anticipated further seemingly unpredictable celestial events, suggesting a force at work with remarkable powers of prediction and one apparently wanting to alert us to perhaps important changes in our

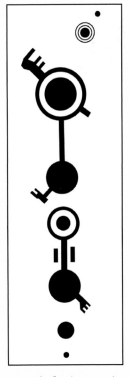

*The first 'pictogram' to gain wide media publicity appeared at Alton Barnes, Wiltshire, on 11 July 1990, and astonished many with what was then an unprecedented complexity*

*Ickleton, Cambridgeshire, 12 August 1991. The first fully identifiable shape to arrive - a 'fractal' known as a Mandelbrot Set*

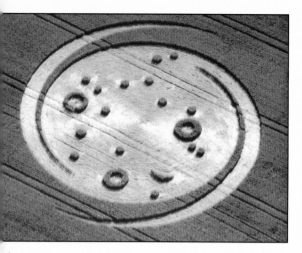

*Two astronomical formations from the mid-1990s.* Left: *The 'galaxy' at West Stowell, Wiltshire, 23 July 1994, showed a planetary alignment due to occur on 6 April 2000 [see text, and chart below].* Right: *Longwood Warren, Hampshire, 26 June 1995; a map of the inner part of our solar system – minus the Earth [see text]! It shows connections with the cycles of Venus and that planet's 'transit' of 2004, though there have also been other interpretations*

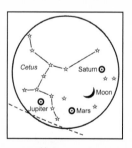

*Diagram showing the actual planetary alignment of 6 April 2000, as indicated in the West Stowell 'galaxy' above*

*Right: A 'Koch snowflake' fractal at Milk Hill, Wiltshire, 8 August 1997*

celestial neighbourhood. 'Asteroid Belt' designs and clear depictions of our solar system, some showing the arrival of comets, and one (Longwood Warren, Hampshire, 1995 – above right) with the Earth mysteriously removed from the map, raised deep questions, showing as it did information on the cycles of Venus (the outer 65 beads denoting that planet's synodic orbital reference points) and the other inner planets in position for 4 June 2004, nine years later, which would be the week of the rare 'transit' of Venus across the face of the Sun. The chart was also suggestive of other dates, depending on how it was read.

1996 saw the return of fractal symbolism in ways that left the Mandelbrot Set looking simple by comparison. The massive Stonehenge formation of 7 July, which appeared by daylight [page 3], was composed of 151 circles, and its amazing triple-armed successor at Windmill Hill, Avebury, on 29 July [page 5] took the number up to 194, with complex and inherently triangular geometry that maintained total accuracy over an area many hundreds of feet across.

More fractal symbolism occurred in 1997 with the arrival of two 'Koch Snowflakes', huge decorative mandalas made up from varied-size repeating triangles, bordered by fringes of tiny circles. By 2000, a quite extraordinary variety of ambitious designs was regularly visiting the fields and now it seemed that any pattern one might think of could appear. In that year, hypnotic and striking optical

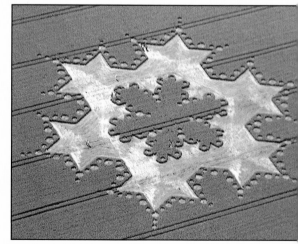

illusion-type formations of criss-crossing arcs staggered many with their breathtaking detail and accuracy.

In 2001 the most impressive crop circle to date appeared, when an 800-feet six-armed motif was discovered at Milk Hill, near Alton Barnes, on 12 August. It contained within it a record-breaking 409 circles, ranging from 70 feet to just three feet across. The pattern arrived on a night of rain, the soil beneath the crop wet and slushy, yet it was found pristine and clean the next morning, with not a muddy footprint in sight. Television crews from around the world moved in on it with a great excitement not seen since the early 1990s. Even a well-known human circlemaker expressed the view that such a vast and complex design could not have been constructed in one night – but it was.

However, the most dramatic development in the evolution of the symbolism thus far came on 14 and 19 August 2001, when two clearly decipherable designs materialised next to the radio telescope complex at Chilbolton, Hampshire. One was an ingenious representation of a humanoid face, made up from small pillars of crop, like pixels, whilst its companion was a

*The enormous 409-circle wheel at Milk Hill, Wiltshire, 12 August 2001. Widely considered the most impressive formation to date, from the ground [below] its vastness made it impossible to discern the pattern*

*The ingenious face and binary message at Chilbolton, Hampshire, 14 and 19 August 2001*

*The binary table is apparently a 'reply' to a message sent into space by the SETI project in 1974. The dot-matrix face resolves into three dimensions when the image is blurred*

rectangular strip, which turned out to be a binary variation on a signal beamed out into space as a test transmission by the SETI project (Search for Extra-Terrestrial Intelligence) to hypothetical extra-terrestrials in 1974 . . . Instead of information describing life on Earth, the Chilbolton 'reply' appeared to show details of life on another planet altogether, with different DNA and alien physiology denoted, amongst other changes.

The inevitable controversy and intense debate which followed these formations deepened further in 2002 when another 'face and message' glyph arrived at Crabwood, near Winchester, Hampshire, on 15 August, a year and a day on from the first of the Chilbolton events. This huge and very cleverly constructed image (this time created with lines of variable width) clearly represented the classic and much-reported 'grey' ET, holding out a disc containing binary code. Astonishingly, the code was rendered in a form known as ASCII (American Standard Code for Information Interchange) – in other words, it was decodable into English text. Translated, it read as a warning, yet it was also a message of hope [see opposite]. A digital bell sound was signified as the final part of the code.

This formation both shocked and amused in equal measure, leaving many to wonder what its true significance was, and who or what we were being warned about, while arguments between sceptics and the now-dubbed 'believers' went into overdrive. Whatever its source and meaning, it was a demonstration of the clear progression in the evolution of the shapes over the years – indeed, this crop design remains the only directly translatable message ever received. Despite specific examples, patterns that are fully identifiable are in the minority, though some plainly present important mathematical tenets, such as the complex wheel which appeared at Barbury Castle on 1 July 2008. This managed to embody the key principles of 'pi' in a way never before demonstrated – thrown down as a free gift, anonymously, in a field! In 2010, another wheel of binary code was discovered at Wilton, Wiltshire, on 22 May, and contained

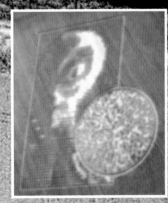

*The controversial but amazing 'ET' and disc formation at Crabwood, near Winchester, Hampshire, 15 August 2002 [see text]. With added blur and contrast, again, the image comes to three-dimensional life [right]. Rendered in a system known as ASCII, the wheel of binary code is set in the English language, and can therefore be read. The exact message follows:*

"Beware the bearers of FALSE gifts & their BROKEN PROMISES. Much PAIN but still time. BELIEVE. There is GOOD out there. We Oppose DECEPTION. Conduit CLOSING"

THE 2012 PROPHECIES
*Around the world, there are prophecies that we are about to enter a period of great and unsettling change. Most famously recorded by the Maya of Central America, but also by many other civilisations and tribes from as far afield as New Zealand, China and North America, the turning of an important 5,125-year cycle occurs on 21 December 2012, at 11.11 a.m. precisely. There is now, naturally, great speculation as to what might transpire around that time. Even aside from the ancient prophecies, some modern astrologers claim the next few years will be ones of great social upheaval and new breakthroughs in conscious awareness. Several crop formations have directly referred to 2012, including this one at Avebury, Wiltshire, on 15 July 2008 — a map of our solar system on 21 December 2012*

within it elements of 'Euler's Identity', a complex equation that links five fundamental mathematical constants.

Although it is true that most crop glyphs remain cryptic and open to personal interpretation, more direct pictorial entries, such as the jellyfish, dragonflies and birds that haunted the fields in 2009 [pages 32 & 46], still materialise from time to time. However, one recurring and very clear theme has made itself known over the last decade – crop formations that refer to historical predictions for the year 2012 [see opposite]. Across the world, several ancient cultures have

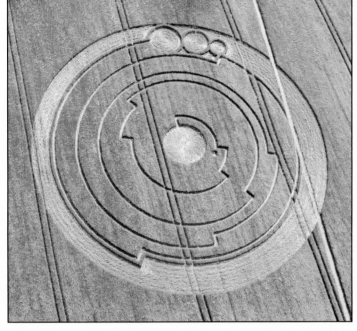

*Barbury Castle, Wiltshire, 1 June 2008 - this complex glyph is a highly accurate diagram that embodies the key principles of mathematical 'pi' - in a way never before demonstrated in human history!*

calendrical systems or traditions based around a time cycle of 5,125 years. Almost certainly derived from some kind of astronomical rhythm (and possibly wider solar patterns), many of the prophecies attached to this period speak of a huge upheaval and transformation that occurs as the cycle ends and begins again, upsetting the old order but leaving humankind in a higher state of being. Excitingly – or worryingly – the turning of the next cycle is due on . . . 21 December 2012, at 11.11 a.m. – the exact moment of the Winter Solstice. Although it is highly likely that this simply denotes the beginning of an era of change (rather than everything occurring on that day), a growing number of people are wondering what is about to happen to our planet – will there be a physical, social or spiritual shift? Or all of these things?

The first clear connection to the 2012 cycle appeared in a formation at Etchilhampton in 1997 (comprising 780 boxes to the value of three Tzolkins – important components of the Maya calendar), and there have been repeated references since, including a diagram based on José Arguelles' depiction of the Mayan '13-baktun cycle' at West Stowell on 20 July 2003 [page 48], a huge wheel of Mayan glyphs at Silbury Hill on 3 August 2004 [next page], and, most strikingly, an accurate map of our entire solar system as it will be on 21 December 2012, which appeared at Avebury Manor on 15 July 2008 [opposite]. In this diagram, only what was assumed to be Pluto was in a deliberately different position, raising much speculation as

*Note this design's similarity to the simpler 'ratchet spiral' on the Barbury Castle triangle of 1991 [page 24], which was in the same field. 2008's version seems to be specifically drawing our attention to the years of symbolic and mathematical evolution in the fields*

This huge mandala at
Silbury Hill, Wiltshire,
3 August 2004, contains
Mayan glyphs amongst
other symbology. It was thus
publicised as 'the doomsday
crop circle' by the Daily
Mail because of its 2012
connections

to which cosmic body it was really depicting – some say it is, in fact, the legendary and long-lost planet Nibiru returning, as predicted in some interpretations of Sumerian myths.

With everything from solar flares, global magnetic field reversals (both of which have been suggested in some crop symbols) and galactic 'superwaves' being discussed as the primary motivators of change from 2012 onwards, many believe we are in for interesting times.

In one school of thought, then, the evolution of the crop designs may have been taking those tuning in on a journey of preparation and consciousness development, to be ready for a new era. Otherwise, at its most basic, we are still left with an extraordinary and wondrous array of quite magnificent art that deserves more attention and respect than it has been given by the mainstream. If the circles continue on, doubtless there will be yet more intriguing and imaginative designs of a nature that no-one can predict. ◎

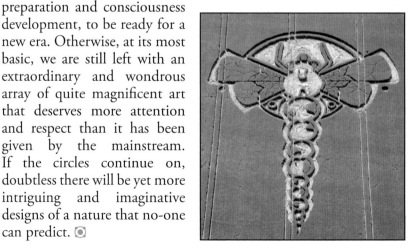

*Right: 2009 saw a spate of circles reflecting nature and lifeforms. This 'dragonfly' at Yatesbury, Wiltshire, 3 June 2009, was seen by some as a positive symbol of new life emerging from its larval stage*

# Crop Circle Development

*A selection of crop formations from past to present, showing the evolution of the designs*

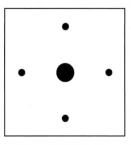

Silbury Hill, Wiltshire,
15 July 1988

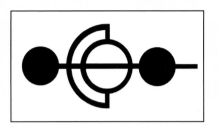

Sompting, West Sussex,
25 July 1990

Avebury, Wiltshire,
11 August 1994

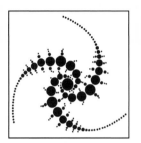

Windmill Hill, Wiltshire,
29 July 1996

Milk Hill, Wiltshire,
8 August 1997

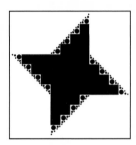

Silbury Hill, Wiltshire,
24 July 1999

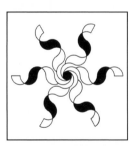

Stonehenge, Wiltshire,
4 July 2002

Avebury Trusloe, Wiltshire,
13 July 2003

Avebury, Wiltshire,
16 July 2005

Waylands Smithy, Oxfordshire,
8 July 2006

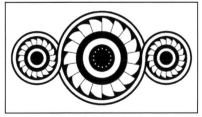

Watchfield, Oxfordshire,
12 August 2008

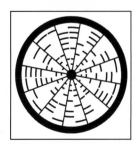

Wilton, Wiltshire,
22 May 2010

*A circle photographer takes a 'pole shot' in the time-honoured way; i.e. a camera is perilously attached to a scaffold pole to gain elevation for pictures*

Hand in hand with the evolution of the shapes has been the development of the research community. Starting with just a handful of dedicated investigators in the 1980s, led by pioneers like meteorologist Terence Meaden, Pat Delgado, Colin Andrews and Busty Taylor, by the 1990s a whole industry of circle-tourists and enthusiasts (or 'cerealogists') had arisen, leading to a rush of books, journals, websites and annual conferences dedicated to the circle phenomenon (the Glastonbury Symposium is the longest-surviving event, still running over 20 years later).

The Centre for Crop Circle Studies (CCCS) was founded in 1990 by other researchers, such as Michael Green, Lucy Pringle, George Wingfield and Michael Glickman, to provide a unified platform for researchers. It served well for a time, forming a network of branches around the UK and some other countries, and helping to nurture new torch-bearers (such as this author) with its sensible protocols and pooled databases. However, perhaps inevitably, holding so many different theories, opinions and personalities under one umbrella proved too much to maintain, and its gradual descent into squabbles, hoax-paranoia and parochialism finally saw the CCCS officially disband in 2005. By this time, however, happily a new generation of cerealogists had arisen (some through global interest stirred by the circle-themed sci-fi film *Signs*, with Mel Gibson, in 2002), which needed only the Internet as its central hub, though other groups, such as the Wiltshire Crop Circle Study Group (WCCSG), continue on successfully today.

Thus a strong (if equally prone to heated controversies and ego-battles) core of faithful 'croppies', linked by forums and websites,

*Waylands Smithy, Oxfordshire, 8 July 2006. A remarkably angular crop circle with barely a circle in it - some researchers interpreted this, ominously, as representing exploding tower blocks*

have kept interest alive over the years, despite all the media debunking. For good or ill, the nature of circle research has, in turn, become less focused on the earlier hands-on measuring and physical examination and has evolved instead into more philosophical and photo-analytical approaches, but participation is at least better available to a wider global community.

*A photographer adjusts his camera for a pole shot, while a mass of visitors explore a crop circle at Alton Barnes, Wiltshire in 2010. On busy days, some formations can have around thirty or forty people in them at any one time! Because of this, they don't stay pristine for long*

For those who do make it to the actual fields, two draws in Wiltshire attract the most enthusiasts: *The Barge* at Honeystreet, near Alton Barnes, although somewhat prone to prowling sceptics, is still a beautiful pub and campsite next to a canal, and hosts a crop circle notice board, but the *Silent Circle Café* has now become the key information point from where to start circle visits. Currently situated at Yatesbury, near Avebury (after moving location at least twice since its beginnings in 2002), it opens during the summer months and is a hive of activity for researchers and circle tourists keen to know the where, when and how of the latest events in the miles of surrounding fields. Eating tea and cake while discussing everything from metaphysics to conspiracy theories, and never being too far from a new circular masterpiece, is something to experience at least once in a lifetime (see *Further Information*).

Some aficionados (inevitably often retired, self-employed or unemployed) spend their entire summers waiting for news of new cereal artworks – or are out looking for them. The more dedicated photographers hire light aircraft or even helicopters on a near-daily seasonal basis to take the aerial shots necessary for the eager armchair cerealogists waiting by their computers. They, in turn, debate on the quality, origins and potential meaning of each new design, pondering long into the night, leaving no stone unturned.

*Not all farmers welcome researchers and may use signs like these to deter them. It may not be an empty threat - in 2009 a scandal erupted when a farm worker fired a shotgun at a group of Norwegian visitors [page 54]*

Every year seems to bring a new generation of entranced devotees to the subject, each one going through their own learning curve of wonder, doubt, amazement and confusion, as many have before them. Some stay, and some go, but all the while the fields continue to provide fresh stimulation, it is likely that researchers, enthusiasts and photographers will continue to dedicate their spare time to documenting this remarkably persistent and entrancing phenomenon. ◉

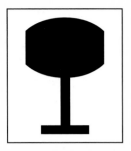

*Hoeven, The Netherlands, 21 August 2001. This design was witnessed being created by bright tubes of light by the only crop circle researcher to date to have had this lucky experience [see text]*

*Woolstone Hill, near Uffington, Oxfordshire, 13 August 2005. Unusual lights were seen in the area the night it arrived. Its 'Mayan' style makes it another formation some have linked with 2012*

Contrary to popular belief, there have been many eye-witness reports from people who have watched crop circles form in front of them, usually within seconds. An intense whistling or 'trilling' sound can accompany this, as can sightings of light phenomena, as previously noted. One account tells of how the witness heard the crop emit a hissing sound, while the seed heads shook violently; then the plants fanned out into a circular shape on the ground, almost within an instant. This occurred on a summer day with no clouds or wind.

In another famous example, in 1989, Surrey couple Vivienne and Gary Tomlinson claim a formation actually swirled around their feet as they were knocked from a footpath into standing crop by a force that took the form of 'mini-whirlwinds' funnelling down from the sky with a powerful sound like 'pan-pipes'. In 2001, US researcher Nancy Talbott (from BLT Research, which co-ordinated much of the biological plant analysis) became the first-ever cerealogist to bear witness to an appearance, as she and a friend watched three tubes of light descend into a bean field at Hoeven, The Netherlands, leaving a steaming ellipse with an emanating pathway [see left].

In recent years, researcher Lucy Pringle has unearthed an important witness to the 1996 fractal formation at Stonehenge [page 3]. A lady claims that, while parked nearby, she watched the circles gradually appearing under a strange mist which hovered over the field. This is an important account, because the formation was so large and complex

(meteorologists have claimed simple whirlwinds could create small circles). Other witnesses have described similar mists forming.

Although there are variations, as illustrated by these examples, in general there is a remarkable consistency to the eye-witness accounts, which convince many of the veracity of the reports. Sceptics insist all such eye-witnesses are liars, but this seems to speak more of blanket rejection than a sensible dealing with facts. Those who don't want to re-write the physics books apparently find it easier to deny than engage.

Just one video exists which purports to show the clear appearance of a crop formation, allegedly taken at Oliver's Castle near Devizes, Wiltshire, on 11 August 1996 [right]. Flying lights are seen to circle over a field as a six-armed snowflake design materialises beneath them within seven seconds. Great controversy still hangs over this footage, with some considering it faked by special effects. However, as yet, despite years of debate and endless claims and counter-claims, nothing has been proven for certain either way. It is in any case an impressive sequence that certainly shows what many have described seeing.

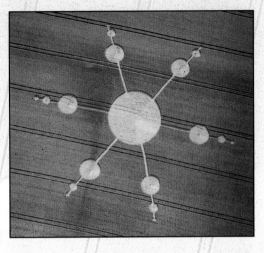

*Oliver's Castle, Wiltshire, 11 August 1996. Possibly the most contentious formation of all time, a video purports to show it appearing under spiralling lights. Many years on and the arguments over the authenticity of the footage, and by default the formation, go on, but the internal swirls were certainly attractive*

Aside from direct daylight sightings, night-time reports of aerial phenomena descending into fields where crop circles are subsequently found are the most common accounts. Some tell of clusters of lights, while other stories describe columns of coloured light shooting electrical charges of some kind down to the ground.

Other examples of bright lights seen in and around existing formations abound, and they have been filmed on a number of occasions. These lights are usually about the size of a football, seen skimming over the seed heads, moving with uncanny precision in some cases, more randomly in others. Balls of light are considered so common around crop circles that some researchers casually refer to them as 'amber gamblers'. Circle-related aerial phenomena can appear in many shapes beyond the usual small lights; cylinders, large spheres and even Ferris wheel-like objects have all been reported. On occasion, lights have been seen to touch the ground softly, rise and float away – crop circles have been found at these sites the next day. Even the 1678 'Mowing Devil' account [page 13] describes aerial lights, suggesting that this aspect has long been a part of the phenomenon.

*Inside the remarkable 'galaxy' [page 26] at West Stowell, Wiltshire, 23 July 1994. Many circle visitors describe peculiar experiences or sightings while walking around them*

*Carl Jung (1875-1961), one of the key thinkers of the 20th century, believed that interest in UFOs heralded a time of great psychological change for humanity. Much of what he wrote in his 1959 book* Flying Saucers *could equally apply to crop circles*

Certainly, what some would call UFOs have favoured the Wessex Triangle region in the recent past. A major UFO 'flap' occurred around Warminster in Wiltshire during the 1970s, attracting international attention. The town even named itself 'UFO Capital of Europe'. Curiously, the phenomenon died down in the late 1970s and instead crop circles began appearing in the county.

The eminent psychologist Carl Jung [see left] wrote that anomalous lights in the sky were harbingers of great changes in the collective psyche, due to occur with the passing of the astrological Age of Pisces into the Age of Aquarius. He believed that the UFOs were actively involved in bringing about the changes. Though Jung saw UFOs more as projections of the mind, many believe the aerial lights and the increasing intricacy of the crop glyphs are an attempt by unidentified intelligent forces to communicate with us – or 'awaken' us.

In addition to lights, unusual sounds have also been reported at crop circles. One in particular, the aforementioned 'trilling' noise, is the most common. Sceptics claim this sound is nothing more than a bird (the 'grasshopper warbler'), but some who have heard it dispute this, and it has been captured on tape for analysis. Crackling, hissing and strange 'knockings' have also been recorded.

We have already seen how circles often have dramatic effects on electronic equipment and physiological effects on visitors [page 10], ranging from feelings of elation, joy, and sudden clarity of thought, to sensations of nausea, fatigue, metallic tastes in the mouth and disorientation. The long list of sightings and anomalous experiences certainly suggests that there is more to the crop circle mystery than just flattened crop. ◉

*There are many potential causes that might account for the crop circle phenomenon, and much theorising has taken place since interest grew from the 1980s onwards. The following possibilities are just a selection of the numerous ideas that have been put forward, but they give a useful overview of the best of the basic concepts which have been discussed over the years.*

## Natural Causes

Biological factors have been known to create very simple patterns in grass, such as 'fairy rings', but there is no known fungus that can create the intricate crop lay and sophisticated patterns seen in some of the amazing pictograms. Lightning strikes and rare whirlwinds are other possibilities which have been suggested, but both tend to leave random destruction. However, meteorologist Dr Terence Meaden postulated the early theory that a 'plasma vortex', an electrically-charged funnel of air, might be responsible for the circles, and some of the plant analysis of W C Levengood backed up elements of this theory, though his BLT Research group felt that a far more complex (and possibly conscious) mechanism must be at work. The vortex idea in its plainest form could only really account for the much simpler patterns, but the finding of very similar techniques at work in both the simple and the complex designs left many questions unanswered. Some argue that there may indeed be a mechanism available in nature that can produce very basic circles by itself (perhaps accounting for the historical accounts), but that something has learnt to harness and enhance the process to create new complexity. This might explain the progression in development seen since the 1980s.

*The science of 'Cymatics' has shown that sound waves passed through mediums like oil or sand can produce incredibly complex patterns. Many crop formations, like these here, resemble cymatics; could there be a link? Top: Avebury, Wiltshire, 14 April 2009. Middle: Windmill Hill, Wiltshire, 2 August 2002. Below: Windmill Hill, Wiltshire, 18 July 2002*

Nature, in general, is very good at producing geometric forms, such as snowflakes, flowers and galaxies. The aforementioned science of fractals [page 25] has demonstrated how chaos theory alone can account for surprising levels of mathematical intricacy, and there have been a significant number of fractal configurations in the fields. Another process that demonstrates the power of nature to 'design' is the art of 'Cymatics', the effects of vibration in physical media such as water, oil and sand. Developed in 1967 by Swiss scientist Hans Jenny, he was

*Wilton, Wiltshire, 22 May 2010. This design embodies elements of a complex mathematical equation known as 'Euler's identity' – though some formations could be of natural origin, patterns like this clearly hint at intelligent design*

able to capture and photograph the exact geometric patterns caused by different sound frequencies. As the frequencies rise, so too does the complexity of cymatic shapes, many of which bear remarkable resemblances to certain crop patterns. Could at least some crop circles be cymatic imprints caused by a change in the natural vibrations of the earth? Many psychic channellers and tribal elders have claimed that the earth is undergoing a change in its 'vibrationary' rate at this point in time (others link this with the 2012 prophecies), and most scientists agree that all matter – including us – is made of vibrating particles. The rising sophistication of the crop circles and people's strong responses to them may indicate an interaction between ourselves and the evolving frequencies of the planet.

Nature alone could surely not account for the clearly intelligent agriglyph designs, astronomical diagrams, binary codes, etc., but it could be responsible for some shapes, and may at least be one component of a much wider process that we do not yet understand.

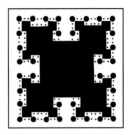

*A square 'fractal' pattern, West Kennett, Wiltshire, 4 August 1999. Not all fractal shapes are circular*

## Earth Energies

Another natural, if more esoteric, force to consider is the theory that crop circles are formed by a planetary interaction with 'earth energies'. From ancient times there has been a belief that an invisible energy network covers the earth ('dragon energy', 'chi' and 'serpent lines', for instance). It has been suggested that quartz and/or underground water may produce this power source, as combinations of these are known to create piezoelectric fields under certain conditions. Underground water, or at least the aquiferous strata it lies in, has long been associated with the placement of crop circles [page 5], and some think that Wilhelm Reich's 1930s 'orgone' energy concept may also be involved. Could this connection be helping to produce formations?

It is claimed that earth energy can be detected through the hands, but the ancient art of 'dowsing' is the most common method. The dowser either holds a pair of rods, usually made of bent wire (though twigs can also be used), or a pendulum. Walking slowly, he or she waits for the rods to start turning or for the pendulum to twirl in a certain direction, indicating that a field of energy has been crossed. Some say that a force acts upon the rods; others insist that the energy affects the dowser, causing minute muscular twitches that can be felt and interpreted. (However, dowsing results can vary from person to

*The late David Russell, an expert 'dowser', at work in a Celtic cross formation at Sompting, West Sussex, 23 June 1993. Using traditional and ancient methods of detection, dowsers claim that crop circles are strong in natural 'earth energies'*

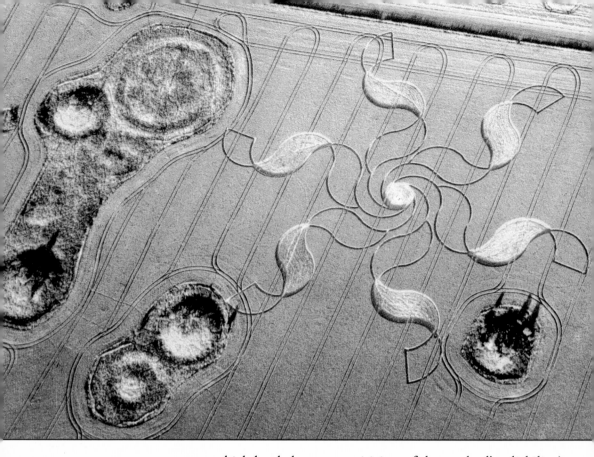

*A beautiful 741-feet diameter design of 'ribbons', perfectly placed between burial mounds near Stonehenge, Wiltshire, 4 July 2002. Many formations cluster near old sacred sites (often stone circles – below), perhaps because ancient Man worked with the same earth energies some believe are involved with crop circles*

person, which has led to some criticism of the method's reliability.)

Certain types of earth energy apparently run in straight courses. These lines sometimes become confused with the concept of 'leys', alignments in the landscape that can most easily be seen by looking at maps and drawing a line through tumuli, burial mounds, churches and other features of antiquity in a join-the-dots fashion. However, some theorise that ancient peoples placed their sacred sites on trails of earth energy, and hence leys may sometimes follow the same course as energy lines. Living in close proximity to the land, and dependent on it for their very lives, maybe early civilisations could feel the power more easily than we can today. This may also explain why crop circles, if connected to this same 'power supply', cluster around so many ancient sacred sites. There is evidence that these lines act as a magnet for light phenomena and other anomalous sightings (including, interestingly, ghosts and religious apparitions). Crop circles often seem to form close to the nodal points of these bands of energy. The two very powerful energy lines known as 'Michael and Mary' are held to run directly through the Avebury area, the region of most crop circle activity.

However, despite the apparent plausibility of particular natural cause and earth energy theories, many formations clearly appear to display intelligent impetus, which leaves the need to consider other explanations that may run in conjunction with this concept.

## Gaia and Ancient Symbolism

The notion that our earth itself may be *choosing* to create the circles is another proposed idea. The Gaia concept holds that the earth is a living, breathing organism, but New Age theory takes the notion a step further to credit our planet with active consciousness. Could crop circles be outward signs of where energy is being intelligently focused, or by-products given off as the earth tries to heal itself? In this school of thought, they could be likened to sore spots, or welts, that can occur on a diseased organism, though their beauty suggests a more positive connotation. Some believe the circles are a premeditated attempt by Gaia to warn us that our destructive, polluting ways cannot be tolerated for much longer before something drastic has to be done; a message from the planet itself.

*Some believe there is an environmental message to certain formations. This 'apple tree' design (or mushroom, upside-down?) appeared at Alton Barnes, Wiltshire, on 15 July 2002*

It has also been suggested that the circles are ancient symbols which appear here and there throughout history at times of need, helping to stimulate our evolution (rather like the black monoliths in Stanley Kubrick's film *2001: A Space Odyssey*). Some Native Americans and other tribal voices have seen the crop glyphs as a cry from the earth, and a portent of coming great changes. A number of groups around the world, not least because of the 2012 prophecies, believe there is an imminent time of global transformation upon us and that the reappearance of these ancient patterns is to help raise our vibrational frequency, even change our DNA, as certain formations that have displayed clear genetic symbolism might suggest.

*Felbridge, West Sussex, 29 June 1995. This simple but distinct formation appeared the very night the Sussex-based Southern Circular Research team (including this author) carried out a meditation with precisely this design in mind. Other groups have also had seeming psychic interaction with crop circles*

## Human Consciousness

The crop circles (or the forces behind them) have on many occasions shown themselves to be responsive to human thought. There have been cases of researchers hoping, privately, to see a certain type of pattern, only to find it the next day. Others have had premonitions and dreams of designs that arrive in reality later. On a number of notable occasions, controlled experiments with the power of the mind have managed to produce particular formations in the fields, seemingly projected from a group consciousness. Shapes have been chosen by small, select groups, and then meditated on, only to then appear as agriglyphs the same day [right]. Aerial phenomena have also been known to interact with observers, as if some kind of psychic link is involved (as Carl Jung asserted - page 38).

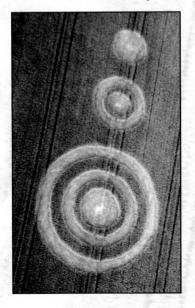

One possible solution to the mystery, therefore, may be that the crop designs are projections from the collective

*Southern Circular Research setting up their successful meditation experiment (at Wolstonbury Hill, West Sussex), 28 June 1995*

*Crop circle enthusiasts seem endlessly fascinated with military activity over crop circles, even when helicopters are merely passing by. Is it only coincidence that the military training area of Salisbury Plain is just a few miles away from the circular epicentre, or is there a more sinister link?*

consciousness of humankind, somehow interacting with natural energy systems to produce shapes in the fields. This could partly explain the apparent randomness of the symbolism, if it is simply a mish-mash of dream-state feedback from the collective mind; intelligent on one level, yet uncoordinated. Experiments such as the ongoing Global Consciousness Experiment [*http://noosphere.princeton.edu/*], begun at Princeton University in the USA, have now demonstrated an ability of focused group thought to affect data produced by computers, and this is being used to show that our minds *do* affect the energetic environment – and who knows what else? – around us. So this theory may not be as unlikely as it at first sounds. What mechanism exists in nature to allow for patterns to be transferred into physicality is currently unknown, and how the likes of the astronomical predictions could be accounted for is less clear, but it is a hypothesis that should not be discounted. Like most circle theories, it raises more questions than answers, but human consciousness may be just one more link in the causal chain of whatever creates the crop glyphs.

## The Military

Some conspiracy theorists have accused the military of creating crop circles by means of energy technology, citing the proximity of army land at Salisbury Plain to the agriglyph sites of Wiltshire, and pointing to the many sightings of military helicopters seen hovering low over formations (although it is likely that some of these events can be put down simply to mischievous pilots-in-training). The less observant have suggested that the downdraft from helicopter blades alone

could account for crop circles, but comparing the mess left by helicopters, which have come too low over fields in the past, with the intricate geometrical beauty of the glyphs leaves this theory as one of the least likely.

Beyond helicopters, what is missing in the military explanation is the nature of the mysterious technology that might be involved and what the motive might be. If it is to test some new weapon or device, why demonstrate it in such public places when there are so many other secret locations that must be available? It has been suggested that the military might be actively researching peoples' reactions to unusual phenomena for some dubious purpose (some hardcore truthseekers believe there is a plan to fake the threat of an alien invasion to help create a mandate for an Orwellian-style global government), but if so, why then invent so many hoaxers and debunkers to so successfully destroy interest in the subject, unless it is all part of a bizarre double-bluff?

The theory that the military make the crop formations, then, is no stronger in logic than many other ideas, though it cannot be entirely dismissed that some may have been created in this way to distract and confuse. (When Colin Andrews and Pat Delgado's televised BBC circle surveillance project in 1990 was duped and discredited by the appearance of a seemingly hoaxed formation [page 49], several pointed out the mysterious coincidence that this occurred on the one night of the project where the military helpers who had been present the rest of the week were absent.) There is certainly evidence that the military is interested in the circle phenomenon, at least, and both the British Ministry of Defence, and Ministry of Agriculture (which conducted soil tests in 1995, identifying an unexplained imbalance in the nitrate and nitrogen levels beneath crop circles – page 51), are known to have quietly maintained their own investigations over the years.

*'Time Tunnel' at Avebury Trusloe, Wiltshire, 30 June 2006. Some believe agriglyphs are tests of secret military technology*

*Martinsell Hill, Wiltshire, 19 July 2007. Is such precise geometry natural or intelligent in origin?*

*Alton Priors, Wiltshire, 8 August 2003, one of several ingenious 'rope' designs. Another appeared at Alton Priors on 22 July 2002 [below]*

*Right: The 'jellyfish', Kingston Coombs, Oxfordshire, 29 May 2009. A number of 'lifeform' designs have appeared over the years. Whilst some mandalas and snowflake-like designs could possibly be of natural origin, ones like this appear to display clear signs of 'conscious' manifestation*

## Intelligent Forces

A significant proportion of crop glyphs strongly suggest that they are trying to tell us something, however obliquely. Could they be, as a large number of researchers believe, a communication from higher beings, be they extra-terrestrial or from other dimensions (or even other times)? The phenomenon has clearly evolved in complexity from year to year in recent decades. Could this be a method of subtle teaching, starting slowly and simply, but gradually increasing the flow of symbolism, feeding us subliminal encoded information to trigger certain parts of our brains?

There have been many cases of strange lights in the sky associated with crop circles, and these have often been interpreted as extra-terrestrial craft, although many sightings seem too amorphous to be conventional solid objects, and some lights seem to act as if they are beings in their own right. There have, however, been more traditional reports of saucer-shaped objects hovering over circle fields, and there is now little doubt that unusual and largely inexplicable objects *do* fly in our skies, wherever they come from, as the increasing amount of supportive testimony from commercial airline pilots, military personnel and even astronauts would seem to confirm. Cover-ups surrounding UFO sightings and claims of alien encounters are very certainly in operation, as anyone attempting to extract direct information from governmental authorities will discover.

But there are many unanswered questions to the intelligence theory. If other beings are trying

to communicate with us, why choose the rather odd medium of writing largely unintelligible graffiti in crop fields? And why not scatter them more evenly around the globe to attract general attention? Why are there so many in England, and yet far fewer in other countries? Is it that the English are of a more conducive mindset than other nationalities to spread the word, or is there a restrictive physical factor at work, such as geology? Why *does* the phenomenon seem to rely on geological qualities to act, and not simply create formations 'from above'? Is it trying to attract our attention to certain important places . . ?

*Etchilhampton, Wiltshire, 11 August 2002; a complex play on the geometrical 'flower of life' concept*

Although the intelligence theory offers more answers than some, it still leaves elusive logic holes to be explained. Some have proposed the notion of a *Star Trek*-like 'prime directive', in which beings that would like to advise or help less-developed races are forbidden to do more than provide tiny nudges. Maybe the crop glyphs are all that is allowed? It may also be that several different kinds of intelligence forces may be involved, and that the symbols do not all come from the same source, as the many different genres and design styles might indicate.

*A 'double-headed serpent' at West Overton, Wiltshire, 23 June 2002. This incredibly perfect spiral is a modern interpretation of a very ancient symbol*

If crop circles do carry some kind of intelligent message (the one-off 2002 'ET and disc' aside), then as yet no one has deciphered the overall code or meaning, despite the quota of

*West Stowell, Wiltshire, 20 July 2003. This is a curious rendition of 2012 researcher José Arguelles' diagram of the Mayan 'thirteen-baktun' cycle, and thus perhaps another pointer that we should be ready for changes to come. It is also the first formation to use 13-fold geometry; not an easy number to use, but rendered perfectly here*

*Beckhampton, Wiltshire, 13 August 2010. An Egyptian symbol, the Holy Grail, or a Roman Catholic host-holder . . ? It is the very mystery of crop circles that has stimulated people in every direction*

recognisable symbols over the years. Could they be transmissions that aren't meant to be intellectually understood, but intuitively instead? Perhaps they use a language of vibration that we subconsciously understand deep within us. The strong reaction from some towards the symbolism would seem to suggest a truth to this. Mathematically, the patterns certainly speak to us with a purity of geometry and form. It is possible that no one message is intended, but that the glyphs are mainly stimuli to encourage our race to greater aspiration and thought, bringing balance between faith and hard evidence and awakening us to be ready for bigger changes to come. Almost uniquely, this is an unexplained phenomenon that seems to speak equally to both men and women and satisfies both 'left-brain' and 'right-brain' thinking, the more masculine elements of physical and intellectual analysis combining perfectly with the more feminine aspects of art and spirituality. This inclusive and welcoming quality has given the crop circles a very wide appeal.

Many of those profoundly affected by the agriglyph enigma have certainly experienced an expansion of consciousness and a subsequent change in their lives, yet it seems clear that this is but a small component in a much wider cycle of global change, deepening self-awareness and a sense of new collective responsibility, which grows year by year.

The bottom line is that the crop circles never deliver answers, but instead continually pose questions in a mélange of multi-cultural, mathematical, astronomical – and totally obscure – designs. Yet it may be that the very inspiration sparked in us to find an answer is the greatest gift of all, stimulating us to expand and evolve ourselves without the need for direct celestial interference.

## Unified Theory

The current truth is that a final answer to the crop circle mystery still remains out of reach despite many years of investigation. Maybe the ultimate solution will lie in a combination of all these different though perhaps not mutually-exclusive ideas. Maybe an answer will never be found, or it lies so far beyond our current understanding and experience that we are simply not ready – nor expected – to comprehend the full meaning or source. The great beauty of the phenomenon has always lain in its mystery as much as in its admittedly breathtaking works of art. It may very well be that it is the fundamental questions and joyous inspiration the crop circles have kindled that matter the most, rather than the answers. ◉

# 9: Crop Circle Timeline

## An at-a-glance guide to circular history

### PREHISTORY
According to speculation based on geometrical and symbolic similarities, some believe crop circles appear in ancient times, inspiring rock art and the building of stone circles on the places of their arrival

### 1600 – 1900
*1678:* The 'Mowing Devil' pamphlet is published, telling of circles appearing in a Hertfordshire field and of demonic events surrounding them – *1686:* In his book *The Natural History of Staffordshire*, Sir Robert Plot writes of unusual 'flattened circles' in local grassland and postulates on mechanisms that might have produced them – *1871:* One William Loosely finds a circular impression in grass and weeds after seeing strange lights at High Wycombe, Buckinghamshire

### 1900 – 1980
*1900-18:* 'Six rings' in a row are reported at Tilshead, Wiltshire. At least two other circles are reported in this period, one in Wiltshire, another in Kent – *1920:* The first US crop circle is recorded, in grass at Mount Pleasant, Indiana – *1920s-50s:* Various remembrances of formations are recorded across the UK (and occasionally other countries), mostly single circles or rings, though a triangle is documented in 1930s' Yorkshire – *1932:* A ring is photographed in fields at Bow Hill, near Chichester, West Sussex (as reproduced in the 1934 *Sussex Notes and Queries* book series) – *1937:* A linear triplet is reported at Helions Bumpstead, Essex. Its appearance within seconds is witnessed – *1943:* Two simple circles are reportedly photographed near the RAF base at Tangmere, West Sussex – *1950s:* The first 'quintuplet' is recorded at Heytesbury, Wiltshire – *1950s-70s:* Various reports of simple formations are documented in the UK and around the world, in countries such as the USA, France and Canada – *1960:* A linear triplet with connecting paths is found at Cheesefoot Head, Hampshire – *1966:* Crop circles are photographed in reed beds at Tully, Queensland, Australia, leading to a spate of Australian 'UFO nest' reports – *1972:* UFO researchers Arthur Shuttlewood and Bryce Bond claim to witness a crop circle forming at Star Hill, near Warminster. Other formations are reported in the area – *1975:* The first 'triangular triplet' is discovered, near Stonehenge – *1978:* The second recorded quintuplet appears at Headbourne Worthy, Hampshire, while the first 'officially-reported' linear triplet is found at Cheesefoot Head, Hampshire [but see 1937 & 1960 entries]

### 1980 – 1988
*1980s:* Sightings substantially increase, and more complexity develops. The first serious investigations are carried out by meteorologists such as Dr Terence Meaden and individual enthusiasts like Pat Delgado and Colin Andrews. Media interest in the phenomenon begins to grow after a 1981 'triplet' – *1984:* Labour politician Denis Healey very publicly photographs a quintuplet near his home at Alfriston, East Sussex – *1986:* The first 'Celtic cross' is discovered at the Longwood estate, Hampshire – *1987:* The first recorded circle with a radial lay is found at Cheesefoot Head – *Late 1980s:* The UK Ministry of Defence reportedly conducts investigations into crop circles and concludes that they are not a man-made phenomenon

### 1989
Vivienne and Gary Tomlinson claim to have a crop circle appear around them as they walk through fields near their home in Surrey (although not reported until 1990) – The first crop circle book *Circular Evidence*, by Pat Delgado and Colin Andrews, becomes an unexpected bestseller and raises the phenomenon's profile enormously – Operation White Crow is conducted by Andrews and Delgado at Cheesefoot Head, Hampshire, the first serious circle surveillance operation. No formation is filmed, but anomalous events are claimed – A 'quartered lay' circle is found at Winterbourne Stoke, Wiltshire, with crop brushed in straight lines, confusing weather theorists and providing an omen of more complex events to follow

### 1990
The Centre for Crop Circle Studies (CCCS) is launched and initialises its journal *The Circular*. Other investigative outfits develop, such as the 'Beckhampton group', which meets at the *Waggon & Horses* near Avebury – The first of the complex 'pictograms' arrives at Chilcomb, Hampshire, to wide astonishment – The new evolution blossoms with large pictograms around Alton Barnes, Wiltshire. Huge media attention sparks international interest and more formations are found in other countries – Delgado and Andrews's Operation Blackbird surveillance exercise, broadcast on BBC 1, is thwarted by the

arrival of an apparently hoaxed design, discrediting the enterprise – Steve Alexander takes the first clear video of a crop circle 'ball of light' at Stanton St Bernard, Wiltshire – The first prototype Glastonbury Symposium is held, an event which will evolve into the longest-running circle-related gathering – *The Cerealogist*, then edited by John Michell, has its first issue

## 1991

US biophysicist W C Levengood carries out the first definitive biological analysis of circle-affected plants, finding unexplained anomalies. This leads to the eventual formation of the BLT Research group – CCCS publishes *The Crop Circle Enigma*, the most comprehensive circular guide so far – The first 'insectograms' and 'whales' appear, pictograms with animal-like features – Three metal plates of almost pure gold, silver and bronze are allegedly dug from beneath a pictogram at Grasdorf in Germany, bearing the same emblem as the pattern itself – Two formations stun researchers: a huge triangular design at Barbury Castle, Wiltshire, and a 'Mandelbrot Set' fractal at Ickleton, Cambridgeshire, ending the era of weather theorising in its basic form – A strange 'ancient script'-like formation appears at Milk Hill, Wiltshire, seemingly in response to the words 'TALK TO US' trampled into crop by a visiting US researcher – In the autumn, two pensioners, Doug Bower and Dave Chorley, claim to have hoaxed most of the formations. Worldwide publicity follows and public interest in crop circles drops dramatically, despite the lack of any definitive evidence – Southern Circular Research (SCR, originally the CCCS Sussex branch) holds its first meeting, and its influential journal *Sussex Circular* appears soon after (edited by this author). SCR/Changing Times will go on to become the longest-running circle group, still active today

## 1992

A series of 'Snail' designs cause controversy with their cartoon-like quality, though many feel they are genuine, despite wide scepticism following the Doug and Dave claims – The Beckhampton research group disbands amidst recriminations and debunker infiltration – The UFO investigation group CSETI meditate on their logo at Oliver's Castle, Wiltshire, and the emblem appears as a formation the next day, a seemingly interactive effect repeated by other groups in subsequent years. CSETI claim to witness substantial UFO sightings over Alton Barnes the same week – A 'hoaxing competition', sponsored by *The Guardian* newspaper and *The Cerealogist*, is controversially held at West Wycombe, Buckinghamshire. Several teams take part, but the variable quality fails to conclusively prove debunking theories – A 'Charm Bracelet' formation appears at Silbury Hill, a complex ring of esoteric symbols. US sceptic Jim Schnabel claims to have made it, but his later public 'recreation' doesn't convince – The first mainstream UK TV documentary about the circles is broadcast as part of Channel 4's *Equinox* series, but is heavily biased towards hoaxing, setting a trend for most TV documentaries since – CCCS's Project Argus releases the results of its scientific investigation, which, though inconclusive, identifies several interesting anomalies

## 1993

'Croppie' culture grows up around *The Barge* pub at Honeystreet, Wiltshire, where both cerealogical enthusiasts and debunkers gather to socialise; or argue – Sceptics work hard to dissuade the faithful, even undermining the personal characters of researchers through rumour-spreading and printed attacks – Jim Schnabel's debunking book *Round in Circles* is published to positive press reviews, but rejection from cerealogists – A complex cross formation appears at Charley Knoll in the East Midlands, seemingly in response to interactive experiments carried out by the local CCCS group – The first design to cross field boundaries arrives at East Kennett, Wiltshire, as a ring encompasses an entire T-junction, in three separate fields – A beautiful 'mandala', the first of its kind, appears at Bythorn, Cambridgeshire, setting a new design trend. Subsequent arguments within CCCS and the holding of a 'trial' to determine its origins split the ruling council, leading to resignations and rifts that undermine the effectiveness of the organisation thereafter

## 1994

Despite beautiful early formations, some UK newspapers declare the phenomenon 'dead', but public interest grows again with the appearance of some of the most amazing designs so far, including 'scorpion'-like pictograms – Unusual ovals at Birling Gap, East Sussex, cause controversy by being laid from halfway-up the stems. Though unhoaxable, some argue they are the work of birds, despite the farmer's denials – 'Galaxy' formations appear, astronomical diagrams of stars and planetary alignments – 'Thought bubble' formations are likened by some to being symbolic representations of comet Shoemaker-Levy 9, the fragments of which collide with Jupiter during the summer – The longest formation yet seen, almost quarter of a mile in length, is discovered at Ashbury, Oxfordshire – A 'web' mandala at Avebury, Wiltshire [page 56], astonishes everyone with its beauty and execution – Pop band Wet Wet Wet have a huge international hit with the old Troggs song *Love is All Around*, propelling its composer Reg Presley into the limelight. His personal passion for crop circles and UFOs thus goes public and renews media interest – W C Levengood publishes his article *Anatomical Anomalies in Crop Formation Plants* in the journal *Physiologia Plantarum*, the first piece on crop circles to appear in a scientific peer-review journal

## 1995

'Asteroid' formations, astronomical-looking charts of orbital rings and clustered 'grapeshot', peak with the remarkable 'missing Earth' design at Longwood Warren, Hampshire, a diagram of our inner solar system, minus the Earth – The 'quintuplet of quintuplets', a Celtic cross made up from four smaller quintuplets, appears at Telegraph Hill, near Cheesefoot Head – A predicted design of circles and rings at Felbridge, West Sussex, appears in apparent direct response to a meditation experiment carried out by members of SCR the same night – Wiltshire has a quieter year, while counties such as East and West Sussex have one of their best – An unusually early harvest effectively ends the UK season at the end of July, with almost no August formations – The Ministry of Agriculture division ADAS [Agricultural Development & Advisory Service] announces the results of soil tests (collected by CCCS) on nineteen formations, showing unexplained imbalances in the nitrogen/nitrate ratios beneath several of them. The department which carries out the tests is mysteriously shut down soon after, sparking dark speculation – The Wiltshire Crop Circle Study Group (WCCSG) is founded from the ashes of the Wiltshire CCCS branch and begins its journal *The Spiral* (still running today)

## 1996

A 'DNA' formation appears at Alton Barnes, resembling a genetic spiral. 'Circlemakers' are invited by the farmer to try to recreate it in the same field, but no-one takes up the challenge – A 915ft 'Julia Set' fractal of 151 circles appears opposite Stonehenge in daylight hours within 45 minutes, according to eye-witnesses who know the time frame in which it arrived. The farmer opens the field to the public and the formation becomes the most walked on record, with an estimated 10,000 visitors – A triple version of the Julia Set appears at Windmill Hill, Avebury, Wiltshire. 194 circles are arranged in perfect geometry of ever-increasing equilateral triangles, maintaining 100% accuracy across an area of many hundreds of feet – The record for the longest formation is set by several circles in a stretched path measuring around 4,100ft in length, at Etchilhampton, Wiltshire (a record still unbroken) – A six-armed 'snowflake' design is apparently videoed as it appears at Oliver's Castle, Wiltshire. It is seen to materialise beneath glowing balls of light within seconds and the video is shown at *The Barge* that day. Savage controversy follows ever after, some claiming it to be a special effects hoax, others defending it as genuine

## 1997

A ring in grass is discovered at Sennen Cove, near Land's End, Cornwall, in January; the earliest annual UK sighting on record – A Qabalah, or 'tree of life', appears as a formation in oilseed rape at Burderop Down, Wiltshire and is seen as a significant symbolic development by some – A hexagonal fractal 'snowflake', the first recorded hexagon, appears next to Stonehenge on precisely the same spot as the previous year's Julia Set, but this time the farmer refuses entry to the public – An increase of formations around the world is reported, with Germany and The Netherlands in particular producing notable designs – Three elaborate triangular-edged 'Koch fractals' appear in Wiltshire, at Silbury Hill, Milk Hill and Hackpen Hill. US surveyors estimate over a week's work would be needed to manually reconstruct the Milk Hill version if operating at night – A grid of 780 small boxes at Etchilhampton becomes the first of several formations to directly reference the ancient time cycle of the Maya and other global cultures, which ends and begins again on 21 December 2012

## 1998

A 'Beltane Wheel' formation appears on 4 May next to the West Kennett longbarrow, comprising thirty-three ingenious 'tongues of flame' – Three of the most sophisticated pentagram designs yet seen arrive, two at Beckhampton, Wiltshire, and another at Dadford, Buckinghamshire – The first ever seven-fold geometry pattern is discovered at Danebury hill-fort, Hampshire, followed by two more extravagant entries in Wiltshire – The second seven-fold pattern, at Alton Barnes, sets the record for the largest single expanse of flattened crop yet found in one component of a formation; more than 6000 square metres – Strange 'larval' motifs and several other 'creature' designs, recalling the 'insectograms' of the early 90s, appear in Wiltshire – A car motif, created by 'The Circlemakers' team for a Mitsubishi advert, reputedly takes two days to construct in daylight hours – There is a burst of press and TV activity, investigating, and making, crop circles – Re-analysis of the 1994 'galaxy' formations by astronomer Jack Sullivan reveals them to be clear predictions of a planetary alignment due to occur in the constellation Cetus on 6 April 2000.

## 1999
Several early formations resemble eclipse symbolism and are seen by many as referring to the total solar eclipse due over the UK in August. A triple-armed spiral at Hackpen Hill, Wiltshire, directly demonstrates the 'Saros cycles' of global eclipse shadow paths – A perfect representation of a Jewish 'Menorah' arrives at Barbury Castle and features in the *Jewish Chronicle* – A serpent design and a long chain of classic pictogram shapes, over 1000ft in length, appear in the same field at Alton Barnes within an hour and a half, according to crop-watchers – An explosion of inventive mandalas incorporating multiple shapes, especially squares and hexagons, peppers the fields of Wiltshire and Hampshire – The then record for the most circles in one formation is broken by a design comprising 288 grapeshot at Windmill Hill – Two clear videos of balls of light are taken on the same day by two different people over the same formation at Barbury Castle – An astonishing 'basket weave' of interlaced swathes is discovered at Bishops Cannings, Wiltshire, but destroyed by the farmer within hours, causing consternation – Many cerealogical enthusiasts witness the 11 August eclipse from within crop formations or sacred sites near circle areas; oddly, the rush of this season's complex designs appears to cease from thereon, as if some kind of impetus has been spent

## 2000
The planetary alignment predicted in the 1994 'galaxy' occurs on 6 April, 'coinciding' with an enormous solar flare, which produces unusually widespread global auroras (seen even over Alton Barnes) and other effects. This raises speculation as to whether some formations are alerting us to important changes in the Sun – A pentagonal design at Alton Barnes begins a spate of 'optical illusion' designs – A gaping hole appears in the top of Silbury Hill, the epicentre of circle activity. Subsidence is responsible, but aerial lights are seen over the hill in the run-up to the collapse, and many believe some kind of 'energy release' occurs, perhaps initiating a new spate of spectacular formations – A Celtic cross at Everleigh Ashes, Wiltshire, encompasses a round barrow, using the mound as its centre, complete with swirled grass and nettles – Colin Andrews announces he now believes 80% of crop formations to be man-made, while the remaining 20% are created by 'natural magnetism'. Little evidence to support either percentage is forthcoming. An incredible 'magnetic fields' design appears at Avebury Trusloe, as if to wryly comment on the Andrews announcement, followed by an astonishingly detailed 'sunflower' sequel at nearby Picked Hill – The first full eleven-fold geometry formation is discovered, at Bishops Cannings, Wiltshire – Michael Glickman discovers that certain formations of 2000, which appear in groups of threes, are arranged to produce near-perfect Isosceles triangles when lines are drawn across the landscape between them, covering areas of several miles

## 2001
Media reports of the first (and only) prosecution of a circle hoaxer promotes renewed scepticism and opens the divisions in the circle community to wider scrutiny – Despite Foot and Mouth disease restricting countryside movement, formations defiantly appear, if slightly reduced in number, though the media obstinately and incorrectly insists that the phenomenon has vanished – Dr Eltjo Haselhoff becomes only the second person to have a scientific paper on crop circles published in the peer-review journal *Physiologia Plantarum* – A stunning 800ft six-armed wheel of a record-breaking 409 circles appears at Milk Hill, Wiltshire, during a night of rain. Media scepticism turns to astonishment and even known hoaxers express doubts as to how it could have been manually created. Huge TV coverage renews wide interest – At Chilbolton, Hampshire, a pixilated humanoid face appears next to a radio telescope, followed by a binary code diagram, apparently a response to a signal beamed into space by the SETI project in 1974. Amazement and controversy follow – Nancy Talbott of BLT Research becomes the first circle researcher to actually witness the creation of a formation, as she and a companion watch three tubes of light descend at Hoeven, The Netherlands, leaving a design in a field of beans – There is a substantial increase of overseas crop circle reports, particularly in Germany – The *Sussex Circular* transfers to the Internet as *Swirled News*

## 2002
The UK experiences the slowest start to a season for many years, with very few events throughout May and June, but things finally pick up in July – A cloverleaf design at Sompting, West Sussex, is discovered with a layer of pure white silica dust coating the central lay. As news spreads, reports come to light of other global formations which have displayed this phenomenon – A 741ft design resembling three-dimensional ribbons is found perfectly poised between three round

barrows near Stonehenge – The release of the movie *Signs*, in which Mel Gibson fends off evil aliens amongst crop circles, creates massive new interest in the phenomenon and a frenzy of media attention around the world. Researchers are kept busy, but debunkers also find an inevitable rise in profile – The popular crop circle-themed café and information centre, *The Silent Circle*, is established at Cherhill, Wiltshire (though it will move locations twice more in the next decade) – Huge controversy is stirred by the arrival of an 'Alien and disc' formation near Winchester, Hampshire. The archetypal ET holding a coded warning message (which translates into the English language) is too much for some, but its construction is remarkable and unmatched by later human attempts to emulate the style – At Crooked Soley, Wiltshire, an astonishing spiralled ring, encoding DNA information, sacred numbers and alchemical connotations, is again destroyed by the farmer just hours after its creation [page 20]

## 2003
A complex mandala appears next to Thornborough Henge, North Yorkshire, a line of three important Neolithic structures. Many researchers see this as a cosmic protest, as the area around the Henge is being threatened with partial destruction by quarrying – Another formation connected with our prehistoric heritage arrives near Bishops Cannings, Wiltshire. The 'Celtic Shield' [page 55] is a remarkably detailed design containing over 400 tiny rings in a concentric configuration, placed perfectly in line with a series of four burial mounds – The first ever 13-fold geometry formation is found at West Stowell, Wiltshire, a complex pattern of radiating diamonds. The design bears a strong resemblance to José Arguelles' diagram of the Maya 13-baktun cycle, prompting further speculation about the 2012 prophecies – The first 'swallows' arrive; bird-like glyphs – With an early harvest in a hot year, UK circle numbers are notably down this year, and almost rivalled by Germany. Italy suddenly receives crop formations for the first time, following its first-ever crop circle conference, and the USA has more reports than usual, though some put this down to *Signs*-inspired pranks – *The Cerealogist* publishes its last issue

## 2004
The slowest start to a UK circle season yet, with just a handful of events by the end of June, though some are stunning. Numbers are generally down around the world – The National Farmer's Union launches a campaign to stop people entering formations, worried about crop damage caused by visitors – An extraordinary winged insect-like glyph is found at Milk Hill, with highly complex geometric properties. A similar, if cruder, design then arrives nearby, but is controversial for developing in stages across several nights – A feeling of gloom is exacerbated by a deluge of media debunking, the antithesis of the *Signs* boom just two years before. However, the UK begins to produce a flurry of remarkable formations again and optimism returns – A 'Mayan Wheel' controversially appears over two consecutive nights at Silbury Hill, a vast mandala of ancient symbols. Because of the Maya/2012 connection, the *Daily Mail* proclaims it as 'The Doomsday Crop Circle' – A formation at Lewisham Castle, Wiltshire, seems to appear in response to an experiment carried out at Alton Barnes, with lights flashed into the sky in binary sequence. It directly references the mystical 'Circle of Nine Points' referred to in the communication, but is also a rendition of the 'Magic Square' representing the Moon's movements

## 2005
A staggering clutch of imaginative formations brings a breath of fresh air and, despite further media debunking, a more positive feel pervades – A design at Alton Priors, Wiltshire, consists only of hard-edged forms, with no circles, surrounded instead by many tiny squares – More traditional elements are taken to new levels at Avebury, with a stunning formation of four Celtic crosses bound together in a striking unified pattern – The first and only (thus far) formation in borage is found at Ludgershall, Wiltshire, the perfect set of concentric rings making for a colourful sight in the blue/purple flowers – Two elaborate mandalas, one at Waylands Smithy, the other near the White Horse of Uffington, both in Oxfordshire, again reference the Maya calendar. Some British newspapers pick up on the 2012-related themes, and the publication of Geoff Stray's *Beyond 2012*, the first complete UK compendium on the subject, helps create growing awareness of 2012 connections with certain crop glyphs – Several countries, such as Germany, go back to basics this year, with simpler glyphs, but Russia has a new spate of formations; local scientists declare them to be the result of 'lightning strikes' – The Centre for Crop Circle Studies (CCCS) finally closes itself down, after a regrettable slide into apathy and disproportionate paranoia over human circlemaking. Few mourn, however, the real research and enthusiasm having long since moved into other, more focused, hands

## 2006

Another very slow start to the UK season and press reports of the suicide of an alleged (if previously unknown) circle artist again give rise to pessimism and yet more media debunking pronouncing the phenomenon, falsely, as dead – Australia and Italy receive the first formations of the year, and Norfolk and Kent activate before Wiltshire. Kent has one of its best years in terms of numbers and quality of designs – A flurry of optical illusion 'time tunnels' appear – A breathtaking mandala of rectangular forms gives the appearance of splayed tower blocks at Waylands Smithy, Oxfordshire. Many formations appear in Oxfordshire this year – A theme of mind-bending 'parabolic' curves emerges at Blowingstone Hill, Oxfordshire, and at Etchilhampton, Wiltshire – Cheesefoot Head in Hampshire reactivates after several quiet years

## 2007

In contrast to the previous year, one of the earliest starts to a full UK season occurs at Oliver's Castle, Wiltshire, on 15 April. It is also the largest diameter oilseed rape design to date, at a mystically teasing 333ft, with an outer ring width of 33ft – An unusual pictorial design depicting a corridor with a chequered floor is discovered at West Kennett longbarrow and fancifully likened to the legendary Egyptian 'hall of records' by some, though others point out its similarity to Leonardo da Vinci's 'Last Supper' – A huge 1,033ft pictogram appears at Alton Barnes [page 56] in front of a night time camera, which records electronic interference at much the same time eye-witnesses report a bright flash over the field around 3.00am, after which the formation is clearly visible after video enhancement – There are increased reports of unusual military helicopter activity over Wiltshire crop circles – Meanwhile, other counties outside Wiltshire and Oxfordshire go mysteriously quiet on circles – Stunning geometrical mandalas of petals and/or three-dimensional-looking 'cubes' are found at Martinsell Hill and Sugar Hill in Wiltshire, respectively – There is an increase in Wiltshire farmers destroying formations as soon as they appear – Global circle numbers go up again, especially in Germany and Italy

## 2008

A beautiful ratchet spiral at Barbury Castle astonishes a US astrophysicist, who identifies it as a way of calculating 'pi', in a way never before demonstrated – An astronomical design at Avebury shows our entire solar system as it will be on 21 December 2012, with only Pluto curiously, and seemingly deliberately, misplaced, leading some to see it instead as the legendary Sumerian 'lost planet' Nibiru on a return orbit – A pictorial design depicts a large glittering jewel at Yatesbury – On 8/8/08, a figure-of-eight configuration of many circles arrives at Milk Hill. Although a mass meditation takes place on the nearby hillside that night, nothing is seen or heard until first light reveals the new design [page 18] – Christian croppies hail an amazing 1,000ft Celtic crucifix design at Etchilhampton [page 56] as a meaningful sign, although others point out that most religions have also been reflected over the years – The UK sees an increase in maize circles, with the largest formation yet found in that medium arriving as late as 28 September – France, virtually untouched thus far, sees an increase in circle numbers, as does Switzerland, while South Korea receives a huge astronomical-style mandala

## 2009

The earliest UK season so far (by one day) begins on 14 April at Avebury, followed by a good momentum of early events – Many designs reflect the natural world, with huge pictorial emblems of jellyfish, dragonflies, birds and even (extinct) trilobites – Several formations grow in stages over subsequent days. One such design at Milk Hill sprouts a huge tail of 'code', hundreds of feet long, containing Mayan references amongst more obscure glyphs – At Alton Priors, Wiltshire, a classic 'ET' face is subtly incorporated into the lay pattern in a section of another code design – Wiltshire farmers step up their campaign of destroying new formations, and conflict with croppies comes to a head when a farm worker fires a shotgun over the heads of Norwegian researchers. The incident makes headline news. The worker is arrested, but only 'cautioned' – Enhancement of a video of an Alton Barnes field on the night a formation arrives shows the apparent materialisation of dark blobs and humanoid figures, leading to speculation over 'co-produced' formations by humans and dark entities – In the Netherlands, the 200th anniversary of the Royal Wilhelminapolder Society is marked by the creation of a vast man-butterfly hybrid crop formation in a Leonardo da Vinci style. Though impressive, the design takes 55 people two days to make, illustrating the extraordinary efforts required to manually construct field art

## 2010

Early formations are a little later this season and ignore the usual areas of Wiltshire to begin with, though they activate again as the summer progresses – In general, there is a wider spread of formations to other counties, with Yorkshire reviving after many fallow years and Warwickshire producing impressive entries – A wheel of binary code at Wilton, Wiltshire, contains elements of the 'Euler Identity', a complex mathematical equation – An extraordinary cubed-cross at Cley Hill, Wiltshire, impresses with a highly three-dimensional effect, ingeniously achieved by cross-hatching some areas of the crop to give 'light and shade' – A new breed of sceptic-croppies claim most formations are now made by the old-time researchers themselves. Unsurprisingly, evidence is not produced – When superimposed one over the other, two 'bead-and-line' formations either side of the M4 motorway at Wickham Green, Buckinghamshire, reveal a cryptic face, which some see as the Mona Lisa and others as the face of Christ – Italy receives its best-ever formation at Poirino, a large and beautiful six-fold floral design of multiple circles – The Glastonbury Symposium celebrates its 21st birthday ◉

# Further Information

*Crop Circle Year Books*, Steve & Karen Alexander, Temporary Temple Press 1999 onwards, around 28pp
*Crop Circles: Exploring the Designs & Mysteries*, Werner Anderhub & Hans Peter Roth, Lark Books 2002, 144pp
*Crooked Soley: A Crop Circle Revelation*, Allan Brown & John Michell, Roundhill Press 2005, 80pp
*Ciphers in the Crops*, ed. Beth Davis, Gateway 1992, 88pp
*Circular Evidence*, Pat Delgado & Colin Andrews, Bloomsbury 1989, 190pp
*Crop Circles*, Michael Glickman, Wooden Books 2000, 58pp
*Crop Circles: The Bones of God*, Michael Glickman, Frog Ltd 2009, 160pp
*The Deepening Complexity of Crop Circles*, Dr Eltjo Haselhoff, Frog Ltd 2001, 157pp
*Mysterious Lights and Crop Circles*, Linda Moulton Howe, Paper Chase Press 2000, 342pp
*Crop Circles: The Hidden Form*, Nick Kollerstrom, Wessex Books 2002, 64pp
*The Circles Effect and its Mysteries*, George Terence Meaden, Artetech 1989, 116pp
*Crop Circles Revealed*, Judith Moore & Barbara Lamb, Light Technology 2001, 265pp
*The Crop Circle Enigma*, ed. Ralph Noyes, Gateway 1990, 192pp
*Crop Circles: The Greatest Mystery of Modern Times*, Lucy Pringle, Thorsons 1999, 144pp
*Crop Circles: Art in the Landscape*, Lucy Pringle, Frances Lincoln 2010, 112pp
*Secrets in the Fields*, Freddy Silva, Hampton Roads 2002, 334pp
*Fields of Mystery*, Andy Thomas, S B Publications 1996, 100pp
*Quest for Contact*, Andy Thomas & Paul Bura, S B Publications 1997, 144pp
*Vital Signs*, Andy Thomas, S B Publications (Frog Ltd in USA) 1998, revised 2002, 192pp
*Swirled Harvest*, Andy Thomas, Vital Signs Publishing 2003, 176pp
*The Truth Agenda*, Andy Thomas, Vital Signs Publishing 2009, revised 2011, 380pp
*The Secret History of Crop Circles*, Terry Wilson, CCCS 1998, 155pp

*Cowdown, Wiltshire,*
*26 July 2007*

BLT RESEARCH: *http://www.bltresearch.com*
CROP CIRCLE CONNECTOR: *http://www.cropcircleconnector.com*
CROP CIRCLE SCIENCE (Andreas Müller): *http://www.kornkreise-forschung.de*
GLASTONBURY SYMPOSIUM: *http://www.glastonburysymposium.co.uk*
LUCY PRINGLE: *http://www.lucypringle.co.uk*
MICHAEL GLICKMAN: *http://www.michaelglickman.co.uk*
THE SILENT CIRCLE CAFÉ: *http://www.silentcircle.co.uk*
SWIRLED NEWS: *http://www.swirlednews.com*
TEMPORARY TEMPLES (Steve & Karen Alexander): *http://www.temporarytemples.co.uk*
THE TRUTH AGENDA (Andy Thomas): *http://www.truthagenda.org*
2012: DIRE GNOSIS (Geoff Stray): *http://www.diagnosis2012.co.uk*
UK CROP CIRCLES: *http://www.ukcropcircles.co.uk*
VITAL SIGNS PUBLISHING (Andy Thomas books): *http://www.vitalsignspublishing.co.uk*
WILTSHIRE CROP CIRCLE STUDY GROUP: *http://www.wccsg.com*

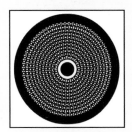

*Bishops Cannings, Wiltshire,*
*6 July 2003*

*Martinsell Hill, Wiltshire,*
*27 July 2008*

# Epilogue

*Barbury Castle, Wiltshire,*
*23 July 1999*

*Etchilhampton, Wiltshire,*
*14 August 2008*

*Avebury, Wiltshire,*
*11 August 1994*

*Alton Barnes, Wiltshire,*
*7 July 2007*

*Knoll Down, Wiltshire,*
*28 July 2002*

Many people drawn to the crop circles have been dramatically affected by their influence. The questioning the phenomenon inspires makes us look beyond the narrow confines of our society and its materialistic obsessions. As a result, some have found themselves on a journey of spiritual self-discovery, or have received mathematical and scientific revelations. Others have become involved in psychic studies, healing, environmental concerns, and even politics. The crop glyphs have opened multiple doorways to new paths, which might otherwise have remained closed to budding explorers without that first kick of inner searching stirred by these beautiful and mysterious shapes.

For some, there has been psychological confusion too, with boundaries of belief uncomfortably stretched. But then what phenomenon so challenging could stimulate only gentle shifts? The battle for reality between the 'believers' and the debunkers has produced a platform for some astounding ideas and forced many to a position of confronting their deepest ideas about the Universe. Some shrink back from this, retreating to the safety of the known, but for those who have embraced mystery and the liberation of uncertainty, the resulting investigation into the *un*known – and perhaps unknowable – has given them many things to be grateful for. One thing is for certain: crop circles have the power to alter a person's life.

No-one knows for sure who or what is making the agriglyphs, neither the mystics nor the sceptics, for all the unproven claims and theories. Our society now bases 'truth' on empirical scientific evidence, and forever ponders on the 'how'. But to answer the circle mystery, should we equally be asking 'why'? And why now? Is the human race being prepared – or subconsciously preparing itself – to experience something huge and profound? Are we on the cusp of a new era for the planet, or are all the 'signs of the times' just a temporary quirk?

Regardless of their origins, the stunning array of crop formations that visit us each summer seem to ignite a wistful longing within those able to see beyond the mainstream's narrow prejudices, alerting us to our almost primal need for the excitement of something bigger than us, outside of our normal experience. With all the advances of modern science and the problems its rigidity can bring, alongside its gifts, it is comforting to know that there are still unexplained and almost impishly elusive areas out there to help balance things, keeping a kind of magic and mystery alive. If all that the circles achieve is to make some souls reassess life itself, the whole venture is surely worthwhile.

What the future will bring in the fields and in our world is anybody's guess. Each year people exclaim 'Nothing can surpass this!', and yet, each year, something does. All, then, that can be expected, is the unexpected, and we should enjoy the journey – while it lasts. ◉